ℙROFILES IN WORLD HISTORY

Significant Events and the People Who Shaped Them

(Continued on inside back cover)

PROFILES IN
WORLD HISTORY

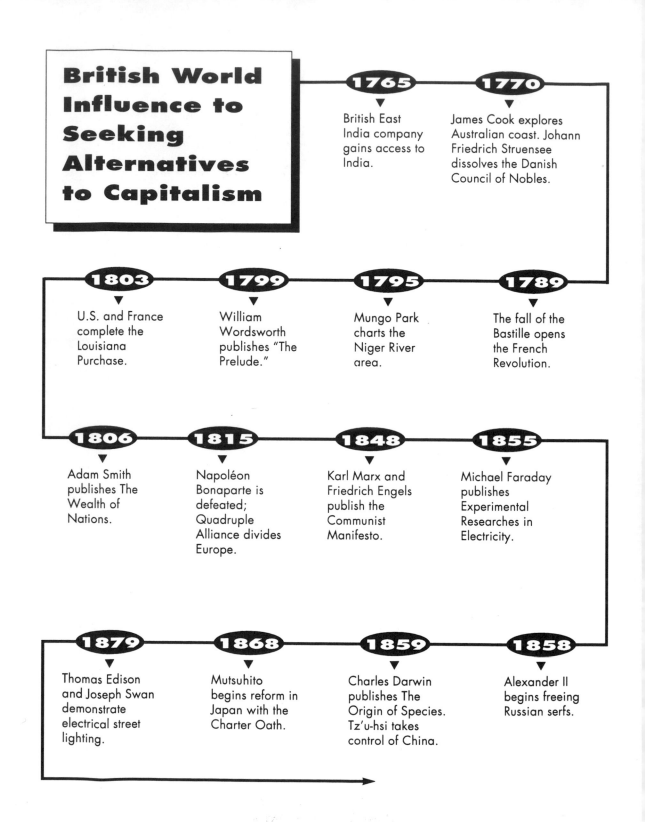

British World Influence to Seeking Alternatives to Capitalism

1765
British East India company gains access to India.

1770
James Cook explores Australian coast. Johann Friedrich Struensee dissolves the Danish Council of Nobles.

1803
U.S. and France complete the Louisiana Purchase.

1799
William Wordsworth publishes "The Prelude."

1795
Mungo Park charts the Niger River area.

1789
The fall of the Bastille opens the French Revolution.

1806
Adam Smith publishes The Wealth of Nations.

1815
Napoléon Bonaparte is defeated; Quadruple Alliance divides Europe.

1848
Karl Marx and Friedrich Engels publish the Communist Manifesto.

1855
Michael Faraday publishes Experimental Researches in Electricity.

1879
Thomas Edison and Joseph Swan demonstrate electrical street lighting.

1868
Mutsuhito begins reform in Japan with the Charter Oath.

1859
Charles Darwin publishes The Origin of Species. Tz'u-hsi takes control of China.

1858
Alexander II begins freeing Russian serfs.

PROFILES IN WORLD HISTORY

Significant Events and the People

Who Shaped Them

5

British World Influence to
Seeking Alternatives to Capitalism

JOYCE MOSS

and

GEORGE WILSON

AN IMPRINT OF GALE RESEARCH
AN INTERNATIONAL THOMSON PUBLISHING COMPANY

℘ROFILES IN WORLD HISTORY

Significant Events and the People Who Shaped Them

VOLUME 5: BRITISH WORLD INFLUENCE TO SEEKING ALTERNATIVES TO CAPITALISM

Joyce Moss and George Wilson

Staff

Carol DeKane Nagel, *U•X•L Developmental Editor*
Julie L. Carnagie, *U•X•L Assistant Editor*
Thomas L. Romig, *U•X•L Publisher*

Shanna P. Heilveil, *Production Assistant*
Evi Seoud, *Assistant Production Manager*
Mary Beth Trimper, *Production Director*

Barbara A. Wallace, *Permissions Associate (Pictures)*

Mary Krzewinski, *Cover and Page Designer*
Cynthia Baldwin, *Art Director*

The Graphix Group, *Typesetting*

∞™ This book is printed on acid-free paper that meets the minimum requirements of American National Standard for Information Sciences—Permanence Paper for Printed Library Materials, ANSI Z39.48-1984.

ISBN 0-7876-0464-X (Set)
ISBN 0-7876-0465-8 (v. 1)   ISBN 0-7876-0469-0 (v. 5)
ISBN 0-7876-0466-6 (v. 2)   ISBN 0-7876-0470-4 (v. 6)
ISBN 0-7876-0467-4 (v. 3)   ISBN 0-7876-0471-2 (v. 7)
ISBN 0-7876-0468-2 (v. 4)   ISBN 0-7876-0472-0 (v. 8)

Printed in the United States of America

I(T)P™ U·X·L is an imprint of Gale Research,
         an International Thomson Publishing Company.
         ITP logo is a trademark under license.

Contents

Reader's Guide

Profiles in World History: Significant Events and the People Who Shaped Them presents the life stories of more than 175 individuals who have played key roles in world history. The biographies are clustered around 50 broad events, ranging from the Rise of Eastern Religions and Philosophies to the Expansion of World Powers, from Industrial Revolution to Winning African Independence. Each biography—complete in itself—contributes a singular outlook regarding an event; when taken as cluster, the biographies provide a variety of views and experiences, thereby offering a broad perspective on events that shaped the world.

Those whose stories are told in *Profiles in World History* meet one or more of the following criteria. The individuals:

- Represent viewpoints or groups involved in a major world event
- Directly affected the outcome of the event
- Exemplify a role played by common citizens in that event

Format

Profiles in World History volumes are arranged by chapter. Each chapter focuses on one particular event and opens with an overview and detailed time line of the event that places it in historical context. Following are biographical profiles of two to five diverse individuals who played active roles in the event.

Each biographical profile is divided into four sections:

- **Personal Background** provides details that predate and anticipate the individual's involvement in the event

- **Participation** describes the role played by the individual in the event and its impact on his or her life
- **Aftermath** discusses effects of the individual's actions and subsequent relevant events in the person's life
- **For More Information** provides sources for further reading on the individual

Additionally, sidebars containing interesting details about the events and individuals profiled are interspersed throughout the text.

Additional Features

Portraits, illustrations, and maps as well as excerpts from primary source materials are included in *Profiles in World History* to help bring history to life. Sources of all quoted material are cited parenthetically within the text, and complete bibliographic information is listed at the end of each biography. A full bibliography of scholarly sources consulted in preparing each volume appears in each book's back matter.

Cross references are made in the entries, directing readers to other entries within the volume that are connected in some way to the person under scrutiny. Additionally, each volume ends with a subject index, while Volume 8 concludes with a cumulative subject index, providing easy access to the people and events mentioned throughout *Profiles in World History.*

Comments and Suggestions

We welcome your comments on this work as well as your suggestions for individuals to be featured in future editions of *Profiles in World History.* Please write: Editors, *Profiles in World History,* U·X·L, 835 Penobscot Bldg., Detroit, Michigan 48226-4094; fax to 313-961-6348; or call toll-free: 1-800-877-4253.

Acknowledgments

The editors would like to thank the many people involved in the preparation of *Profiles in World History.*

For guidance in the choice of events and personalities, we are grateful to Ross Dunn, Professor of History at the University of California at San Diego, and David Smith, Professor of History at California Polytechnic University at Pomona. We're thankful to Professor Smith for his careful review of the entire series and his guidance toward key sources of information about personalities and events.

We deeply appreciate the writers who compiled data and contributed to the biographies: Diane Ahrens, Bill Boll, Quesiyah Ali Chavez, Charity-Jean Conklin, Mario Cutajar, Craig Hinkel, Hillary Manning, Lawrence Orr, Phillip T. Slattery, Colin Wells, and Susan Yun. We'd especially like to thank Jamie Mohn and Cheryl Steets for their careful attention to the manuscript.

Thanks also to the copy editors and proofreaders, Sonia Benson, Barbara C. Bigelow, Betz Des Chenes, Robert Griffin, Rob Nagel, and Paulette Petrimoulx, for their careful attention to style and detail. Special thanks to Margaret M. Johnson, Judith Kass, and John F. Petruccione for researching the illustrations and maps.

And, finally, thanks to Carol Nagel of U·X·L for overseeing the production of the series.

Picture Credits

The photographs and illustrations appearing in *Profiles in World History: Significant Events and the People Who Shaped Them,* Volume 5: *British World Influence to Seeking Alternatives to Capitalism* were received from the following sources:

On the cover: **The Granger Collection:** William Wordsworth, Thomas Alva Edison; **The Bettmann Archive:** Tz'u-hsi.

©**Anthony Wolff/Phototake NYC:** p. 122; **AP/Wide World Photos:** pp. 91, 178; **Archive Photos:** p. 10; **The Bettmann Archive:** pp. 70, 84, 111, 139, 173, 192; **The Granger Collection:** pp. 2, 18, 23, 25, 34, 37, 45, 47, 79, 89, 105, 109, 117, 118, 127, 129, 142, 147, 153, 159, 164, 166, 181, 184, 189, 201, 209; **Kunsthistorisches Museum, Vienna:** p. 55; **Library of Congress:** pp. 15, 60, 69, 101, 211; **Photograph by Jonathan Liffgens:** p. 58.

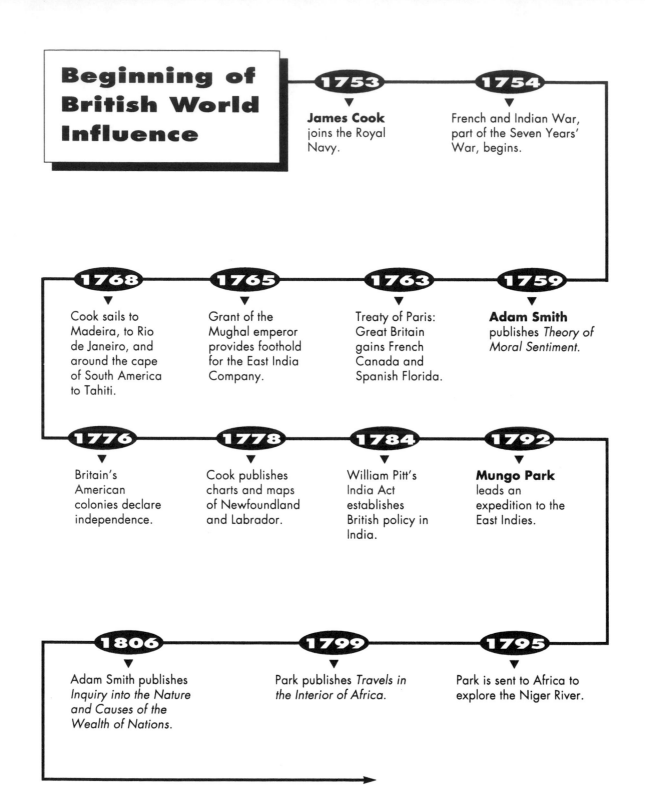

Beginning of British World Influence

1753
▼
James Cook joins the Royal Navy.

1754
▼
French and Indian War, part of the Seven Years' War, begins.

1759
▼
Adam Smith publishes *Theory of Moral Sentiment.*

1763
▼
Treaty of Paris: Great Britain gains French Canada and Spanish Florida.

1765
▼
Grant of the Mughal emperor provides foothold for the East India Company.

1768
▼
Cook sails to Madeira, to Rio de Janeiro, and around the cape of South America to Tahiti.

1776
▼
Britain's American colonies declare independence.

1778
▼
Cook publishes charts and maps of Newfoundland and Labrador.

1784
▼
William Pitt's India Act establishes British policy in India.

1792
▼
Mungo Park leads an expedition to the East Indies.

1795
▼
Park is sent to Africa to explore the Niger River.

1799
▼
Park publishes *Travels in the Interior of Africa.*

1806
▼
Adam Smith publishes *Inquiry into the Nature and Causes of the Wealth of Nations.*

BEGINNING OF BRITISH WORLD INFLUENCE

In 1588 the British navy (along with a terrible storm) destroyed Spain's invading fleet of ships, the Spanish Armada, giving Britain dominance of the sea. Soon British ships were trading on all the continents. Also during the sixteenth century the Renaissance spread across the channel from Italy to France to Scotland and finally to England, leading to a flourishing in the arts and sciences. By the beginning of the eighteenth century the zeal for knowledge in the British Isles was matched by the zeal of British traders, who were demanding more and more goods for trade abroad. Other nations sought their share of this new wealth as well, prompting fierce competition for trade and means of production, and even fiercer nationalism. Every nation strove to dominate the new markets and resources opening up around the world.

What made a nation great? The common notion was that national greatness was measured by how much gold and silver was stored in the state coffers. British rulers followed this principle, and British explorers sailed everywhere in search of wealth that could be exploited for the good of Great Britain. They visited remote islands and continents and established bases in Australia, Africa, and India. **Mungo Park** investigated the possibilities for generating British wealth in the East Indies and then turned

1

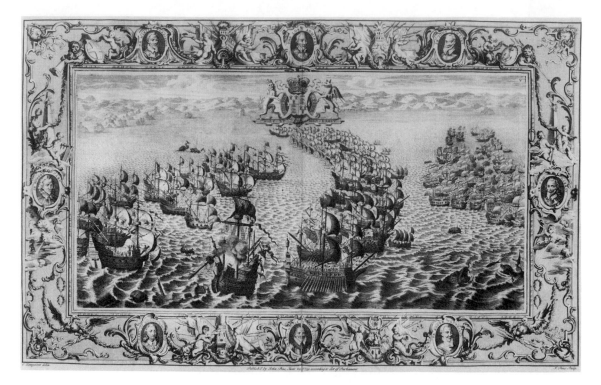

▲ **After the British navy destroyed the Spanish Armada in 1588, British ships were trading on all the continents.**

toward West Africa. There, assigned to explore the Niger River, Park established British influence in what is now Nigeria and Benin. About the same time, **James Cook** set out for the East. Sailing west, he stopped at Rio de Janeiro in South America and then rounded the Cape of Good Hope to land at Tahiti, later to chart the Australian coastline.

Not all of the British territories settled for the role of suppliers to the British merchants. The British colonies in America were eager to acquire wealth for themselves and demanded more and more independence from England. Their restlessness came to a climax at the end of the Seven Years' War (American French and Indian War). The colonists thought it only right that Britain should protect them in this conflict and they resented British demands for repayment after the war. But the war had been expensive, and the British Empire was determined to regain the reserves of gold and silver that had marked it as the dominant empire in the world.

Some British disagreed with this notion, however. **Adam Smith** refused to recognize gold and silver stores as the mark of wealth. Just as the American colonies began fighting outright for independence, he released a book detailing his economic theory. A nation or empire is not rich because of its hoard of gold, he said, but because of its ability to produce materials for market. Smith pushed for absolutely free enterprise and for very little government involvement in economics. Government, he said, should confine itself to such necessities as protecting its citizens from foreign invasion. Smith's book about how nations acquire wealth spread new economic ideas throughout the West, in much the same way that England had spread its influence on local governments during its quest for colonial land and riches during the same period.

James Cook

1728-1779

Personal Background

A dream of the sea. James Cook was born in November 1728, in a small, land-locked farming community in Yorkshire, England. His father, James Cook, Sr., was an uneducated farmer who had been industrious enough—and good enough with numbers—to become the manager of a neighbor's farm. By the standards of eighteenth-century rural England, there was not much more a lower-class farmer could ever expect out of life.

But young James did expect more. Although he had only a few years of formal education at the village school, it was clear that he had inherited his father's mathematical abilities. In his early teens, dissatisfied with the drudgery of farm life, he set out for the town of Staithes, a fishing village that offered more opportunities. In Staithes he became the apprentice of a dry-goods merchant, and for several years he sold dry goods and drapery; during that same time, he watched the ships come and go, and dreamed of becoming a sailor.

It was a preposterous dream, and Cook knew it. He was already seventeen years old and had spent most of his life on a farm; apprentice seamen started their careers at the age of twelve or thirteen and were expected to be experts by his age. But Cook decided to try. After an argument with his master at the dry-goods store, his apprenticeship there was canceled. Cook moved to

▲ **James Cook**

Event: Charting the globe and claiming territory for Britain.

Role: Captain James Cook chose the life of a seaman, becoming first a fighter in the British war with France and then an explorer who opened the South Pacific to British trade and settlement.

Whitby, ten miles south of Staithes. Whitby was a large commercial port on Yorkshire's North Sea coast reputed to have the best sailors in all of England.

A late start. Cook spent more than a year trying to get an apprenticeship on a ship in Whitby. His persistence finally paid off, though, when two elderly Quaker brothers named Walker signed him on to one of their cargo ships, the *Freelove.* The *Freelove* was a wide, flat-bottomed ship called a "cat," which hauled coal. The *Freelove* would sail down the coast of England full of coal, navigating the Thames River to energy-hungry London. There it would unload and sail back to Whitby, empty. In his three years as an apprentice, Cook made countless trips to London. In his spare time, he studied mathematics and taught himself the highly valued skill of navigation. Because of his intense interest in seamanship, he excelled in it and became a valued member of any of the crews he worked on.

Apprenticeships in Eighteenth-Century England

Because formal education was so rare, jobs requiring any specialized skills or knowledge were learned by apprenticeship. Instead of a salary, apprentices received bed and board for their labor and slowly learned the trade they hoped one day to master. Legally, all apprenticeships ended at the age of twenty-one; thus, apprenticeship in the more difficult trades started earlier.

Cook worked for the Walker brothers for nine years. During this time, he served on four ships and was promoted from apprentice to able seaman to mate. In 1755, when he was twenty-seven, Cook was offered the final promotion—to command his own Whitby cat for the Walkers. To everyone's astonishment, Cook turned down the offer. Even more surprising, he quit his job and joined the navy as a volunteer seaman.

A military career. Cook's decision was startling, to say the least. To be *pressed* into the navy was the worst thing that could happen to a seaman. British sailors were taken from the lowest classes and treated poorly. Nobody with Cook's abilities ever volunteered. To Cook, however, the navy offered greater adventure and opportunities for advancement, especially in the summer of 1755. Britain and France were fighting an undeclared war, and it was becoming evident that the next theater of operations would be across the Atlantic, in Canada.

Cook's first assignment was on the *Eagle,* a sixty-gun ship whose rigging was in need of much work. Cook made such an impression upon the captain that he was promoted within weeks to the rank of petty officer. The *Eagle* was put on blockade duty, patrolling the coast from Land's End to Ireland's Cape Clear, looking for French commercial vessels. That October, the captain was replaced by an exceptional officer named Hugh Palliser, who recognized Cook's ability and promoted him to the rank of bos'n (short for "boatswain")—a high-level petty officer. At this rank, Cook was given command of his first ship in the spring of 1756. The ship was a small one, a cutter, which was assigned to sail alongside the *Eagle* and extend its patrolling ability.

When the weather got better, the *Eagle* and its entourage saw more action as more French ships tried to slip through the blockade. Sometimes the French surrendered outright. Other times, they were captured only after battle. Eventually the *Eagle* got into a prolonged battle with a French gunboat, the *Duc d'Aquitaine,* that nearly destroyed both ships. The French vessel was ultimately captured, but the *Eagle* had to return to Plymouth for

> ### Cook as a Mapmaker
>
> When Cook's map of the St. Lawrence was completed, it was so accurate that it didn't need to be revised for more than a century.

repairs, and its crew was laid off. Through the intercession of Palliser, Cook was offered a naval commission—command of his own gunboat. On his twenty-ninth birthday, and after only two and a half years in the service, Cook was appointed to the sixty-four-gun *Pembroke.* Moreover, he was heading off to fight the French in North America.

Quebec. The siege of Quebec was a lengthy undertaking. The British decided upon a three-pronged attack on French Canada, the most important part of which was a direct naval assault on Quebec by way of the St. Lawrence river. Success depended upon a thorough, yet secret, mapping of the river in advance of the attack. This task fell into Cook's hands. Every night for a week, Cook led a small group up the St. Lawrence, charting the fast and deadly river. The group braved Indian attacks, the difficulty of working in darkness, and the peril of unknown waters to complete the work.

One night in September 1759, the British fleet finally made their advance up the St. Lawrence. Every ship arrived in Quebec safely, and the attack was successful. The following year, Cook published his New Chart of the River of St. Lawrence, which made him well known as an expert mapmaker and navigator. Although he kept a house in London and spent the winters there, he was still working for the navy. For the following seven years, while Palliser was governor of Newfoundland, Cook surveyed the coasts of Newfoundland, Labrador, and the surrounding regions. During this time, he also became more knowledgeable in the field of astronomical navigation. The results of his investigations were published in England, and his fame continued to grow.

Cook and the Royal Society. By 1766 Cook had been commissioned to command the schooner *Grenville*. In July of that year, he took the *Grenville* on an expedition to the coast of Newfoundland to observe a predicted solar eclipse. The observations were sent back to England and were eventually published by the Royal Society.

The society, whose aim was to encourage science, soon had another mission; eighty years earlier, the astronomer Edmond Halley had predicted that the planet Venus would cross the sun's path in 1761 and again in 1769. Knowing that the 1769 transit would be most visible over the South Pacific, the society petitioned King George III to finance an expedition there. The king agreed to pay the expenses and even offered a navy ship for the voyage. While the king himself was interested in promoting science, England also had practical (political and economic) reasons for exploring the Pacific; France, England's long-standing enemy, was already sending expeditions to that little-known part of the world.

Exploration of the South Pacific. Any Pacific expedition of this time had several goals. European countries were mainly interested in establishing colonies, discovering new peoples with whom to trade, and finding viable shipping routes to get there and back. Finally, there was the intriguing question of *Terra Australis Incognita,* the great "missing" southern continent. Cartographers had long been troubled by the enormity of the South Pacific, and they reasoned that there must exist a great land mass to "balance" the amount of known land in the Northern Hemisphere. Australia and New Zealand were known, although their details were sketchy; in any event, they weren't considered large enough landmasses. Locating *Terra Australis,* or disproving its existence, was also an important goal of any expedition to the South Pacific.

Participation: Charting the Globe and Claiming Territory for Britain

Cook's first voyage. Since the Royal Society was familiar with Cook's work as a navigator, they accepted Palliser's suggestion that he command the voyage to the South Pacific. Cook was promoted to the rank of lieutenant and preparations began. Tahiti, in the South Pacific, was chosen as the island from which to observe Venus's transit. A former Whitby coal cat, the *Endeavor,* was modified for the trip. This was an unusual choice of ship for such an expedition, but Cook was able to convince the Royal Society of its practicality for the job. On August 26, 1768, the *Endeavor* sailed out of Plymouth with ninety-four scientists, marines, and crewmen.

Cook sailed southward, past the western coasts of Europe and northwestern Africa, and crossed the Atlantic to South America. The *Endeavor* stopped at Rio de Janeiro but crew members were not allowed ashore unescorted because the governor there thought they were spies—a reasonable suspicion, considering that there were no coal cats in the British Navy. Unwelcome, they stayed only long enough to get supplies; they'd been at sea for ten weeks already and knew it would be a year or more before landing at another civilized port. From Rio, the *Endeavor* followed the eastern coast to the southernmost tip of the continent, stopping briefly at Cape Horn. The ship was so close to the South Pole that a dog and several crewmen froze to death overnight.

Tahiti, the island paradise. In early April, the ship reached Tahiti, where the crew was greeted by Polynesian natives who rowed out to meet them. Friendly relations were established, and the *Endeavor* sailed around the island to the north shore, where they set up camp. A temporary observatory, called Fort Venus, was built and guarded relentlessly; although the natives

▲ **Cook and his crew being met by New Hebrides natives; some Polynesians would row out to greet Cook's ships.**

were good-natured and eager to trade, they were also constantly stealing the expedition's supplies. Cook, knowing how easily the situation could deteriorate, tried to keep a cool head about the thievery. Only when an irreplaceable quadrant—necessary for astronomical measurements—had been stolen did he take drastic action. Cook held several chiefs for ransom until the instrument was returned.

Despite this and other occasional incidents (crewmen deserting the ship to be with their native girlfriends, for example) general order was maintained long enough to observe the transit of Venus in early June. Having accomplished their primary goal, the crew of the Endeavor set sail again. This time they headed south, in search of *Terra Australis.*

Terra Australis. In October, Cook reached New Zealand. Again Polynesians met the *Endeavor* by canoe. Unlike the natives of Tahiti, however, the inhabitants of New Zealand initiated out-right warfare and were subdued only after witnessing the superiority of cannons over spears. For six months, the *Endeavor* sailed around New Zealand, discovering that it was composed of two distinct islands. Cook mapped its 2,400 miles of coastline and dispelled the earlier belief that it might be part of a larger land mass. Parties of scientists made frequent trips ashore, collecting unusual plants and animals to bring back to England.

When New Zealand had been charted to Cook's satisfaction, he claimed the islands in the name of the British Crown and decided to head home. The *Endeavor* had already been at sea for two years, and Cook thought it unwise to continue looking for *Terra Australis* with the winter months approaching again. He decided on a westward course back to England, a course that would circumnavigate the globe.

In April 1770 the *Endeavor* reached the southeast coast of Australia, and Cook decided to follow the coast northward. At the end of the month they reached a large natural harbor, and dropped anchor there for a week. When his scientists reported finding many unknown plant species in the area, Cook named the harbor Botany Bay. During their stay, his crew caught giant stingray in the bay, which they ate.

Leaving Botany Bay, Cook continued northward. He continued mapping the coast of Australia until the *Endeavor* struck a coral reef that punctured its hull. In this way, Cook unwittingly discovered the Great Barrier Reef, a dangerous twelve-hundred-mile-long coral formation off the coast of Australia. The *Endeavor* was forced to return to shore for repairs, this time at the mouth of a river. The repairs took six weeks, until the end of July. By this time, the spirit of exploration had given way to a desire to return home. Cook went ashore on Australian land just once more, to take possession of New South Wales for England. Then the *Endeavor* left Australian waters for the long trek back to Europe.

The *Endeavor* reached England on Saturday, July 13, 1771, with a wealth of scientific data, maps, surveys, and a collection of plants and animals never before seen in Europe, including a kangaroo. But one of the primary objectives of the voyage, the discovery of *Terra Australis,* had not been accomplished. It was inevitable that the Royal Society would organize another expedition in search of the continent, and there was no doubt as to who would command it.

Cook's second voyage. Almost exactly one year after returning home Cook was off again, this time with two ships in his command, the *Resolution* and the *Adventure.* Cook decided that sailing around the South Pole would guarantee his discovery of *Terra Australis,* if it existed at all. He reached Cape Town, South Africa, in November 1772, and continued southward until his ships crossed the Antarctic Circle the following January. It was the first time this had ever been done.

In October 1773 a storm had separated the two ships off the coast of New Zealand. The *Adventure* returned to England, leaving Cook with only the *Resolution.* A month later, he headed southward again to complete the circumnavigation of Antarctica. This feat was accomplished by February 1774, although Cook may not have realized it at the time. For the following year and a half, the *Resolution* continued to chart South Pacific Islands, and, weather permitting, the Antarctic. Cook sailed through all the expanses of ocean he missed on his first voyage, becoming more and more confident that there was no great southern continent. At one point, he became terribly sick and almost died. Still, the *Resolution* continued its expedition, until Cook was certain that *Terra Australis* did not exist. When he returned to England, three years after he left, the American Revolution was underway.

Aftermath

The Northwest Passage. Cook's third and final expedition left England in July 1776. This time he went in search of a Northwest Passage over North America. Such a Northwest Passage had been sought before, but only from the eastern side. Cook thought his chances for finding it were better if he approached from the west. Again, he took the *Resolution,* and another ship called the *Discovery.* He sailed south from England to Cape Town, then east across the bottom of Africa and Asia, stopping again in New

Zealand, Tahiti, and Hawaii before sailing northeast. Reaching the coast of what is now Oregon by the beginning of March, his ships followed the west coast of North America, passing present-day Seattle and Vancouver. By July Cook reached the Aleutian Islands. Northward, he found nothing but an endless expanse of ice. Since this was the warmest time of the year, he knew that this ice never melted; there was no Northwest Passage.

Death in Hawaii. Cook headed south to spend the winter in Hawaii, which he reached in January 1779. Although the Hawaiian natives were initially friendly, thievery immediately became a problem. A fight broke out between his crew and the natives, and Cook was stabbed to death on the beach at Kealakekua Bay on February 14, 1779.

In his three voyages, Cook dispelled the myths of a great southern continent and the existence of a Northwest Passage. Because of his tremendous navigational intuition, he discovered sea routes that opened up the South Pacific as a viable destination. His stunningly accurate maps provided geographic clarity to replace the vagueness and conjecture that had existed before him. These contributions were essential to the British aim of controlling the region, a control which was not long in coming; nine years after Cook's death, the settlement of Sydney was founded in Australia. Soon England would be able to say, with no exaggeration, "The sun never sets on the British Empire."

For More Information

Cameron, Roderick. *The Golden Haze.* Cleveland: World Publishing, 1964.

Moorehead, Alan. *The Fatal Impact.* New York: Harper and Row, 1966.

Villiers, Alan. *Captain James Cook.* New York: Charles Scribner's Sons, 1967.

Adam Smith

1723-1790

Personal Background

Early life. Adam Smith was born on June 5, 1723, at Kirkcaldy, a town located a few miles north of Edinburgh, Scotland. His mother, Margaret Douglas Smith, had grown up in the nearby town of Leslie. His father, also named Adam, was a lawyer and judge advocate of Scotland. He died a few weeks before his son was born.

Adam grew up surrounded by relatives and cared for by his mother. Except for one incident, his early life seems not to have been too different from the lives of other young children around him. That incident occurred when he was three years old. He was taken on a visit to an uncle's house in Strathendry, and he was playing alone there when he was picked up by group of travelers reported to be tinkers (shapers of metal). His absence was quickly discovered, however; his kidnappers were quickly run down, and the boy was recovered in a nearby woods.

From 1729 to 1737 Adam attended the Kirkcaldy grammar school, where he studied under the very able teacher, David Müller. At school, Smith revealed a liking for books and seemed to have a remarkable memory. He did well in his studies but also found time to be popular with his classmates. Growing up in Kirkcaldy, a seaport, Smith encountered sailors, miners, customs officials, nail-makers, and smugglers. In his writings as an adult, he would refer to all of these professions.

▲ **Adam Smith**

Event: Beginning an economic revolution.

Role: Adam Smith, an economist and philosopher, attacked the protection of market trade through government regulations and promoted a free-market economy in his book *The Wealth of Nations*.

▲ Glasgow University; at the university Smith studied under Francis Hutcheson, a professor of moral philosophy and a social reformer who delivered his lectures in English rather than the customary Latin.

College student. In 1737, at the age of fourteen, Smith entered Glasgow University, a small but influential college. Here he showed particular interest in mathematics and philosophy. His interest in philosophy led him to study under Francis Hutcheson, a professor of moral philosophy and a social reformer who pressed for free speech and individual freedom and who delivered his lectures in English rather than the customary Latin. In later years, Smith's writing and lecturing style would reflect Hutcheson's influence.

After winning a scholarship to Oxford University in 1740, Smith departed for England on horseback, leaving Scotland for the first time in his life. He was not at Oxford long before he began to feel that the faculty was incompetent and lazy. He found the whole learning climate at Oxford to be dull. Consequently, Smith studied a great deal on his own and spent much of his time in the library.

Mathematics at the university was particularly backward. Unable to find a professor learned enough to instruct him in that subject, Smith turned his full attention to philosophy and history. In addition to Latin and Greek, he learned French and Italian in order to read ancient and modern literature on these subjects.

Lecturer. Disappointed by his experience at Oxford, Smith returned to his mother's home in Kirkcaldy in 1746 without completing his studies. For the following two years, he looked for work. He soon made the acquaintance of Henry Home, a leading Edinburgh lawyer, who was impressed by Smith's intelligence and education. Home arranged for Smith to give a series of lectures on rhetoric and literature. These lectures were not part of any college program but were popular with law and religion students as well as with prominent Edinburgh citizens. Smith was well paid for his lectures.

University teacher. Smith's lectures boosted his reputation as a scholar, and he soon attracted the attention of officials at Glasgow University who appointed him professor of logic in 1751. The following year he became professor of moral philosophy, taking over the chair once held by his former professor Francis Hutcheson, author of *A System of Moral Philosophy*.

Smith taught courses in political science, law, moral philosophy, writing, logic, and rhetoric, lecturing in English as had Hutcheson. He also held a number of administrative positions at the university while, at the same time, writing a book of his own on moral philosophy. This first book, published under the title *The Theory of Moral Sentiments*, was widely read and acclaimed. The Irish statesman Edmund Burke called it "rather painting than writing" (West, p. 80). Scottish poet Robert Burns was said to have read and valued the book.

Tutor to the duke. The book brought Smith to the attention of Charles Townshend, who introduced crop rotation to British

▲ Taking issue with the mercantilists, Smith contended that the wealth of nations was determined not by its gold and silver but by the productivity of its labor force.

agriculture. Townshend was stepfather and guardian of Henry Scott, Duke of Buccleuch. He offered to pay Smith £300 a year—two-and-a-half times his salary as a college professor—plus a £300 pension for life if he would serve as tutor and traveling companion for his teenage stepson. Smith accepted the offer, resigned from the university, and in 1764 departed with the duke for France, where he would remain for the following twenty-eight months.

In France, the two traveled extensively, allowing Smith to make acquaintances among the cultural and intellectual elite. He soon, however, began to miss his friends in Scotland. Therefore, in 1766, after the duke's brother died, the duke returned to London and Smith returned to Kirkcaldy.

In 1767 Smith again took up residence in his mother's home. He would spend the following nine years writing a new book. On March 9, 1776, *An Inquiry into the Nature and Causes of the Wealth of Nations* was released by a London publisher.

Participation:
Beginning an Economic Revolution

Smith's economics. In his book, Smith presented both an analysis of economics and a series of policy recommendations. Using historical and contemporary examples, he explained the principles of economics and, in particular, why some nations were wealthy and others were not.

Mercantilism was a popular economic theory after the decline of feudalism. It was based on national policies that involved creating a merchant marine, developing colonies, and exploiting mining and industry to accumulate national wealth. Smith argued strongly against this philosophy. Mercantilists believed that a nation's wealth depended on the size of its gold and silver reserves. These were maintained or increased by a favorable balance of trade, or selling more goods to foreign nations than were purchased from them. According to mercantilist thought, nations could only become wealthy at the expense of others. In keeping with this philosophy, governments imposed restrictions on economic activity that included controls on exports, imports, wages, prices, and interest.

Taking issue with the mercantilists, Smith contended that the wealth of nations was determined not by its gold and silver but by the productivity of its labor force. Increasing productivity demanded a division of labor so that each worker involved in a project did what he or she could do best. In his book, Smith illustrated this principle with a description of the manufacture of pins. A single worker working without machinery, he argued, "could scarce ... make one pin a day," but when each worker in the process of pin-making is assigned a specific task—one straightening the wire, another cutting it, a third worker pointing it, and so on—ten men can make forty-eight thousand pins a day (Smith, pp. 8-9). The effects of a division of labor, Smith argued, can be further enhanced by the development of machines and by making improvements in technology.

Smith noted that societies dependent on hunting and fishing, where there is little division of labor, tend to be the poorest, whereas industrialized nations, where there is considerable division of labor, are the wealthiest. Furthermore, the division of labor arises from the human "propensity to truck and barter" (Smith, pp. 8-9), which, in turn, is stimulated by self-interests, including a desire for economic gain, a love of ease, and a fear of punishment.

Thus, Smith saw self-interest as the basis of all economic activity. Even though with everyone working to promote self-interests, the economy might appear chaotic, Smith argued that each individual seemed to be led by an invisible hand toward promoting the public interest. It is not from the kindness of the butcher, the brewer, or the baker that we expect our dinner, Smith suggested, but from their regard to their own interest. Still, in serving their own interests, butchers and bakers also served the community.

With all economic action driven by self-interest but nevertheless guided toward the public interest, Smith outlined his view of the role of government. The proper role, he felt, was to protect society from foreign invasion, control crime, and provide some public services such as maintaining roads. Smith strongly opposed government involvement in economic matters, and much of the book is devoted to attacks on mercantilism and its restrictions. He contends that absolute economic freedom would be far more effective in promoting a nation's wealth than controls on commerce aimed at accumulating reserves of gold and silver.

Smith's book attacks other practices as well. He denounces slavery because it is economically inefficient, and he contends that imperialistic policies only benefit a few businessmen and colonial officials while taxpayers pay the bill for maintaining an empire. Smith admired the American colonies for their free trade policies and self-rule, which he contrasted with the autocratic policies of the Spanish Empire and the British East India Company. He thought the American colonies should be given virtual independence.

Aftermath

The book. *The Wealth of Nations* won acclaim soon after its publication and became a best-seller. The book was widely read in continental Europe and in America. Thomas Jefferson and Alexander Hamilton were among Smith's admirers. The book, which has been in print continuously since 1776, remains a fundamental text for those championing free-market economics with limited government intervention.

Adam Smith. In 1777 Smith was appointed commissioner of customs at Edinburgh. He spent much of his time reading Greek poetry, meeting with other prominent citizens and scholars at Edinburgh social clubs, and holding receptions and parties in his home. He remained a lifelong bachelor.

Additional works. Although he talked of producing additional works on philosophy, science, law, and government, none of these were completed before his death. Smith was sixty-seven when he died in July 1790. A week before his death, he had the manuscripts for his unfinished works burned.

For More Information

Glahe, Fred R. *Adam Smith and The Wealth of Nations.* Boulder, Colorado: Colorado Associated University Press, 1978.

Raphael, D. D. *Adam Smith.* Oxford, England: Oxford University Press, 1985.

Smith, Adam. *An Inquiry into the Nature and Causes of the Wealth of Nations.* Chicago: University of Chicago Press, 1976.

West, E. G. *Adam Smith.* New Rochelle, New York: Arlington House, 1969.

Mungo Park

1771-1806

Personal Background

Mungo Park was born in Scotland on September 11, 1771, the seventh in a family of thirteen children. He was raised in a three-room house in Foulshiels, a small sheep-farming town near Selkirk. Despite the cramped living situation, the family was sufficiently well-off to afford a maid and a private tutor, who schooled the children while their parents tended the farm. Even as a small child, Mungo had ambitions of greatness. One day, as he watched the maid sweeping up pages which had fallen from a book, he told her that someday she would be sweeping up pages from his book.

By the time he started attending grade school in Selkirk, Mungo was already taking long walks through the country, alone. He developed a reputation for being shy and interested mainly in his studies. At the same time, he was obsessed with the idea of becoming famous. When his father suggested that he become a priest, Mungo thought it was too boring. Instead, he wanted to be a surgeon.

At age fourteen Mungo moved in with a school friend in Selkirk whose father, a surgeon, offered Mungo an apprenticeship in the field. An apprenticeship in surgery for a relatively poor boy like Mungo Park was a cheaper way of getting into medical school than an expensive private education. His apprenticeship

▲ **Mungo Park**

Event: Exploring the continent of Africa.

Role: By venturing alone into the unknown interior of West Africa, Mungo Park was the first modern European to see the Niger river. His observations helped cartographers to fill in the blank spaces on the African map and spurred future interest in the development of British commercial interests in West Africa.

and his high grades got him admitted to the medical program at Edinburgh University in the fall of 1788. He was seventeen.

During his four years in medical school, Mungo lost his interest in surgery and developed a new one in botany, the study of plants. Finishing school in 1792, Mungo immediately moved to London, where his brother-in-law, James Dickson, was becoming known as a botanical expert. Because of the family tie and their strong mutual interest, Mungo was frequently at Dickson's North London home. It was through Dickson that he met Sir Joseph Banks, president of the Royal Society, Britain's most important science organization, and a fellow botanist.

Mungo?

The name Mungo was fairly common in the Park family; it was the name of the traveler's father and of one of his cousins as well. St. Mungo was the patron saint of Glasgow, but it was nevertheless a highly unusual name, even for a Scotsman.

The African Association. Four years earlier, over dinner at St. Alban's Tavern in London, a dozen members of the English upper class started discussing Africa. They lamented how, while the rest of the world was being explored, mapped, and commercially exploited, the deep interior of the vast African continent was still a mysterious unknown. European contact with Africa was limited to the regions north of the Sahara, Dutch-inhabited South Africa, and the western coastal areas. That evening, the twelve diners decided to start an organization called the African Association to add to the general knowledge of Africa through discovery of the great African interior.

Instead of a grand commercial effort, the association felt that their mission would be best accomplished by one man with an explorer's heart and a scientist's head. Such an expedition would be quicker and cheaper than previous ones, and ultimately more successful—provided they found the right man.

Early attempts. During its first four years of operation, the association had managed to send three explorers to Africa. The first, an American named John Ledyard, went to Egypt, planning to walk south from there to Nubia and then westward across the continent. Unfortunately, Ledyard never made it out of Egypt; he died in Cairo in 1788.

▲ A watercolor of Park, circa 1805, by Thomas Rowlandson; Park's observations helped cartographers to fill in the blank spaces on the African map and spurred future interest in the development of British commercial interests in West Africa.

The second explorer, Simon Lucas, began his journey in North Africa from Tripoli. He was never able to penetrate the interior, and another explorer had to be found. The third, Major Daniel Houghton, was able to get further than either of his two predecessors. His letters referred to places and peoples that British cartographers of Africa had never heard of. On the whole, though, Houghton never provided enough details, and the African map remained vague. In Houghton's last note, dated September 1, 1791, he wrote that he was on his way to Timbuktu. He was never heard from again.

By 1794 the African Association was hard-pressed to find a fourth volunteer. Then the organization's treasurer, who happened to be Sir Joseph Banks, remembered Mungo Park the botanist. Park had just returned to Britain from the East Indies, where he had been working as an assistant ship's surgeon. When Banks contacted him about the proposed expedition, Park immediately returned to London for an interview. When the association accepted him, Park wrote a letter to his brother, telling him he was going to be famous. His instructions were simple: to reach the Niger and ascertain its course and termination, and to explore the principal cities nearby—especially Timbuktu.

Participation:
Exploring the Continent of Africa

Park's first expedition. Park arrived at the west coast of Africa in June 1795, in the town of Jillifree at the mouth of the Gambia river. He made his way inland along the river, passing through several tribal kingdoms, taking mental notes of everything he saw and heard. Near the ocean, the Gambia was full of sharks. Further inland, he started to see crocodiles and hippos. He soon met up with a European trader named Dr. John Laidley, who brought Park further up the river to his settlement, Pisania.

Pisania was a slave trading post, located north of the Gambia in the Niani kingdom. Although Park was horrified by Laidley's treatment of his slaves, he spent five months at Pisania, learning the Mandingo language and waiting for the rainy season to end. At the end of July, he came down with a fever, which incapacitated him for several months.

After a slow recovery, Park headed due east to Segou, which was either a kingdom or a city, or both. In any event, it was near the Niger river, the goal of his expedition. From there, he would follow the Niger to a town called Jenne, which was supposed to be en route to the mysterious city of Timbuktu. After that, his only further objective was to survive long enough to return to England with his accounts. With no roads or signs to guide him, his method of travel was simple: to head in the general direction of his destination, and ask directions whenever possible. Laidley provided two guides. One of them, a black man named Johnson, had lived in London for seven years and was fluent in both English and Mandingo. The other man was a young slave who could speak Serahuli. In addition, Park brought a compass, two pistols, an iron pot, a blanket and a change of clothes, and some cloth, amber, and tobacco for bartering. It was a light load for such a long journey, but Park was optimistic that he needed no more. On December 2, 1795, the twenty-four-year-old Park set out with Johnson and the translator for the African interior.

Soon, the party entered the city of Medina, the capital of Wuli. Park was surprised at the size of Medina; with nearly one thousand houses, the town was twice as big as Selkirk. Park was greeted warmly by the king, who put him up for the night and offered him a guide through his kingdom. The next morning, however, the king tried to dissuade Park from continuing further inland. He had thought about it the previous night and had decided that warfare, robbery, and persecution of Christians by Muslims made further exploration by a lone European too dangerous. Park thanked him for the concern but moved on.

Eventually the group reached Fatteconda, the capital of Bondu. Once there, Park followed the local custom for foreign traders, which was to wait at the public square until invited into someone's house. It took the townspeople some time to come out and welcome them and, even then, they were not greeted warmly.

From Fatteconda, Park traveled northeast into considerably less friendly territory, entering Khasso on December 28. Once he reached the capital, Koniakary, he was received warmly by the

Seasoned Traveler

In those times, Europeans who caught their first fever in Africa had roughly equal chances of dying outright or surviving and developing a partial immunity to future illness. The Europeans, who knew nothing about the causes of these fevers, called the process "seasoning." Parks survived his first attack and thus was "seasoned."

king—and advised of the dangers ahead. Nevertheless, Park and his party continued to Kaarta, whose king confirmed that an invasion from the southern kingdom of Segou was underway. Park was advised to leave the area for the duration of the war but he insisted on a risky journey, through the very hostile Moorish kingdom of Ludamar.

Captured by Moors. Soon after crossing into Ludamar on February 18, 1796, Park and his group were seized by its Moorish inhabitants. Moors, the nomadic Arab Muslims who occupied that desert region, were known to be ruthless in their dealings with travelers, especially to Christians. Once captured, Park began to fear that he would die before reaching his goal.

For five months, Park was the prisoner of the Moors, traveling with them and enduring their harsh treatment. He was constantly taunted and accused of being a spy—of scouting the African interior for a future European invasion—and he was frequently delirious from hunger and thirst. Still, escape seemed too risky, until he heard of an impending invasion from Kaarta. At that point, escape seemed to offer the best chance for survival.

Early on the morning of July 2, Park and Johnson fled. Johnson would go no farther, but Park insisted on continuing his journey toward Segou, through which the Niger supposedly flowed. Despite the fact that he had been robbed of everything he owned, he refused to give up when he was so close to the Niger. The two parted company and Park, after several days and several close calls with hostile Moors, was out of Ludamar.

By the time he reached Segou, Park's appearance was extremely shabby and destitute. No one could even believe he was European any more, since Europeans were supposed to be rich, and he was obviously very poor. His clothes were so worn that even slaves were embarrassed to be seen with him. Nevertheless, he was treated kindly by the tolerant people of Segou, who eagerly brought him to the bank of the Niger on the morning of July 21, 1796. He immediately saw that the river flowed eastward, settling that question once and for all. Segou, as it turned out, was the name of both the kingdom and the city on the banks of the Niger. The city itself was enormous on both sides of the river, with ferries perpetually shuttling people back and forth.

Park counted several mosques and estimated the population at thirty thousand.

Having found the Niger, Park got a canoe-lift downstream to Silla, three hundred miles northeast of Segou. There, he discussed his plans with traders and local inhabitants, who gave him gloomy news. The regions downstream of Silla, including the city of Timbuktu, were controlled by fanatical Muslims. Making matters worse, the rainy season would be starting again, making further travel impossible except by boat. Since he couldn't afford boat travel, having nothing left to barter with, he decided to turn back and head home. His last night in Silla, he tried to learn as much as he could about the course of the Niger. When he asked the locals where the river went, they told him that it ran to the world's end.

The long road home. On July 30, 1796, Park began his long journey back to England. He was robbed several times and often accused of spying; he almost died from a second bout with fever. This left him stationary for seven months in the town of Kamalia, where he was cared for by a Muslim slave trader named Karfa. When Park recovered, and when the rainy season ended, he traveled with Karfa by caravan back to Laidley's camp, Pisania. They arrived there on June 10, 1797, one and a half years after Park first left the camp.

The next day an American ship docked in a nearby town, with tobacco and rum to exchange for slaves. Park decided to take it. The ship sailed on June 17, but due to a lack of essential provisions, it didn't leave Africa for another four months. Park finally landed at Falmouth, England, on December 22, and arrived in London on Christmas morning.

Park settles down. Park spent much of the next year in London, writing the story of his travels and working with a cartographer to reconstruct the African map from his observations. In July 1799 he married Allison Anderson, whom he had known for a long time; she was the nineteen-year-old daughter of the surgeon Park lived with in Selkirk.

That same year, Park published his account of his expedition, entitled *Travels in the Interior Districts of Africa*. The book was an immediate best-seller, and although Park became quite famous for his work, the central questions were still unanswered: Where did the Niger begin? Where did it end? The answers to these questions would have great commercial value, for if the Niger did empty into the Atlantic, it opened the prospect for ships to sail into the remotest regions of Africa. After Park's expedition, the next step would be to return to the Niger and sail downstream to locate its termination.

Park desperately wanted to resume the life of an explorer and actively sought another mission from the African Association. But the association had no plans for further exploration, and Park eventually realized he would have to find a more conventional job. In September 1801, at his father-in-law's urging, Park set up a surgeon's practice in the Scottish town of Peebles.

The second expedition. After two years in Peebles, Park was beginning to settle down. He and Allison had three children, and his surgery practice was providing solid income for his family. His hopes for returning to Africa were starting to fade, too, as the African Association seemed increasingly unlikely to fund another expedition. When interest in such a venture was renewed, in fact, it was by the British government's Colonial Office.

The British were concerned about the expanding French presence in West Africa and wanted to establish its own colony in the region. To that end, the Colonial Office proposed a river voyage down the Niger, led by Park. Park accepted the offer and was made a captain so that he could effectively command the expedition. Park chose his wife's brother Alexander Anderson as his second-in-command, and the two men left England in January 1805.

By April the entire expedition was assembled. In addition to Anderson, Park brought thirty-five soldiers and two carpenters, who would supervise the construction of a boat once the group reached the Niger. The party traveled by boat up the Gambia River to Kaiai, where they disembarked. Here, they acquired the services of an African trader named Isaaco, who agreed to join them as far as the Niger.

Park decided upon a course to the Niger that followed the return route from his previous trip. With his small army behind him, he had no fear of robbery, but the large size of the party made the voyage slow, and the expedition soon encountered serious problems. Bee swarms, dysentery, food poisoning, and the onset of the rainy season decimated their number. By the time Park reached the Niger, after three and a half months in Africa, only ten of his men were still alive. Since the carpenters were among the dead, the remaining explorers had to buy canoes for their trip downstream. In addition, they had to repeatedly obtain permission to travel on the Niger, which became more difficult the further they went. These obstacles considerably slowed their voyage on the Niger, and by the time they arrived in Sansanding on October 2, fever and dysentery had claimed more men. Park stayed in Sansanding for one and a half months, waiting for additional supplies.

Finally, on November 19, 1805, Park was ready to resume his journey down the Niger. By this time, his entire party had been reduced to himself, three soldiers, and a few slaves. After writing a few letters home, his expedition left Sansanding in a makeshift boat. What happened to Park subsequently, no one knows. He was never heard from again.

Aftermath

Rumors of Park's death began to reach the coast within the year, and conflicting accounts leave some doubt as to whether he ever saw Timbuktu. The most widely believed theory is that Park was attacked in April 1806, as his boat passed through the rapids at Bussa, and that he drowned while trying to escape.

Although Park never realized the ultimate goal of his mission, his observations allowed subsequent Europeans to finish his undertaking; twenty-five years after his death, John and Richard Lander completed Park's exploration of the Niger, traveling from Bussa to one of its outlets at Bass. Today, the event is commemorated at the Park-Lander Memorial, on the bank of the Niger at Jebba, in present-day Nigeria.

For More Information

Bennett, Norman. *Africa and Europe*. New York: African Publishing, 1975.

Hallett, Robin. *The Penetration of Africa*. New York: Frederick A. Praeger, 1965.

Lupton, Kenneth. *Mungo Park, the African Traveler*. New York: Oxford University Press, 1979.

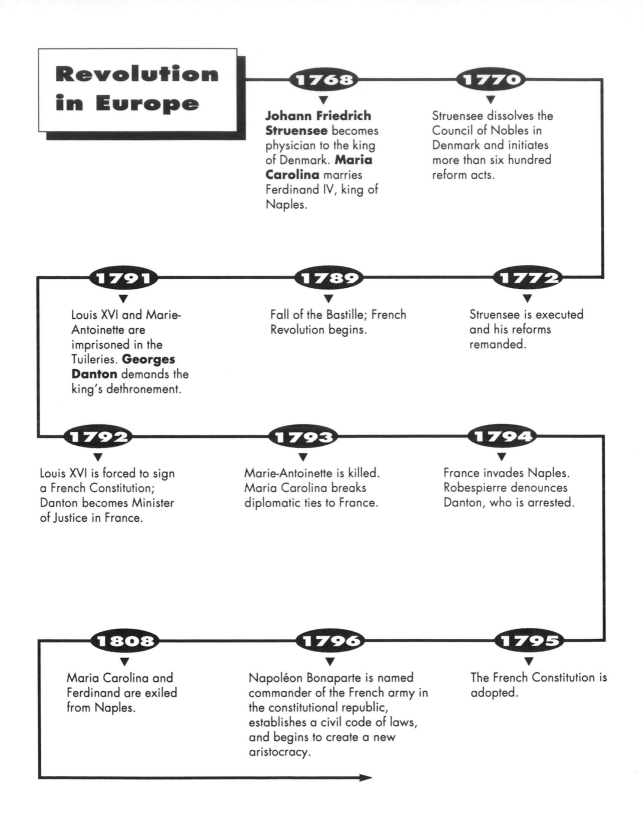

Revolution in Europe

1768
▼
Johann Friedrich Struensee becomes physician to the king of Denmark. **Maria Carolina** marries Ferdinand IV, king of Naples.

1770
▼
Struensee dissolves the Council of Nobles in Denmark and initiates more than six hundred reform acts.

1791
▼
Louis XVI and Marie-Antoinette are imprisoned in the Tuileries. **Georges Danton** demands the king's dethronement.

1789
▼
Fall of the Bastille; French Revolution begins.

1772
▼
Struensee is executed and his reforms remanded.

1792
▼
Louis XVI is forced to sign a French Constitution; Danton becomes Minister of Justice in France.

1793
▼
Marie-Antoinette is killed. Maria Carolina breaks diplomatic ties to France.

1794
▼
France invades Naples. Robespierre denounces Danton, who is arrested.

1808
▼
Maria Carolina and Ferdinand are exiled from Naples.

1796
▼
Napoléon Bonaparte is named commander of the French army in the constitutional republic, establishes a civil code of laws, and begins to create a new aristocracy.

1795
▼
The French Constitution is adopted.

REVOLUTION IN EUROPE

French philosopher and writer Voltaire was a principal leader of the Enlightenment and vigorously urged reform in autocratic European governments. Imprisoned for his views in France's infamous Bastille prison several times, he was finally exiled to England. He arrived there at a time when that country was becoming one of the most powerful and wealthy nations in the world. Returning to France after two years, he wrote about the contrasts between the two countries. He was enchanted by what he perceived to be much greater individual freedom in England. His writings stirred Europeans to think about and demand a better way of life. Another writer, Jean-Jacques Rousseau, joined Voltaire in calling for change. These two, perhaps more than any other of the "philosophes," a band of French philosophers, started Europe on the way to reform and rebellion.

Evolution or revolution? The ideas of these revolutionaries spread across the continent, and citizens became committed to making the changes they suggested, even if it meant offending the nobles who controlled feudal Europe. A few rulers began to see the suffering of the poor in their countries and to view the rule by nobles as an obstacle to progress. For some time before the 1770s, rulers had measured their strength more by the amount of gold and silver they had hoarded than by the happiness, welfare, and productivity of their subjects. Although some

▲ The storming of the Bastille during the French Revolution; the fortress prison of Paris was more a symbol of monarchic power than a source of weapons.

countries began reform early, the struggle for individual freedom was nowhere fought so violently, and possibly nowhere as futilely, as in France.

Reform in Denmark. Johann Friedrich Struensee, a German, was inspired by the revolutionary ideas of the Enlightenment and became committed to change. If only he could reach the throne of Denmark, he thought, changes would soon occur. Using his training as a physician and his personal charm, Struensee earned a position as physician to the king of Denmark and a favored status with the queen. By 1770 he had, with the queen's help, taken the responsibility of government from the weak king. Within less than a year, he enacted reform after reform—more than six hundred—that improved the lives of the Danish serfs. But the Danish nobility was not prepared for this change. For his troubles, Struensee was tried, convicted of treasonable acts, and executed. Nevertheless, reform throughout Europe could not be stopped.

Reform in Naples. An Austrian noblewoman, **Maria Carolina,** daughter of Maria Theresa, was, as was the custom among royalty, married off at an early age to the king of Naples (who was also to become king of Sicily). Although only fifteen when she reached Naples, Maria Carolina soon took complete charge of the kingdom, replacing her uninterested husband, Ferdinand IV. Maria Carolina was a benevolent ruler, constantly trying to diminish the power of the nobles and to improve the lot of the poor. She had hospitals erected for the poor, gave them food, and began to free some of them from oppressive serfdom.

It was not enough. By the late 1780s and early 1790s the rebel groups that were forming in France had become organizers in Italy and Naples. The constant threat to what Maria Carolina believed to be a kindly rule finally turned her into a tyrant. She organized her own secret police and began throwing those even slightly suspected of wrongdoing in jail. Maria Carolina was eventually replaced by a renewed Ferdinand, who proved to be even more tyrannical, and finally by the dictator who rose out of the smoke and fire of the French Revolution to conquer much of Europe, Napoléon Bonaparte.

The French Revolution. Voltaire and Rousseau had lit the fire of revolution, but no one fanned the flames more vigorously than **Georges Danton.** A very large man with uncommonly unhandsome and even frightening features and a booming voice, Danton became the symbol of the bloody rebellion that turned violent with the fall of the Bastille in 1789. He was an uncompromising man; nothing, not even a new constitution, would satisfy him except to get rid of the king and queen forever. He lived to see the two rulers beheaded and the rebellion turn to chaos. It was the chaos he had helped create that finally resulted in his own arrest, conviction, and death.

The French Revolution seemed to burn out the fuel for reform. Soon a dictator would be in charge of France, and the nobles of Europe would return to even stronger positions of autocracy. It would be many years before calmer heads would prevail and the ideas of the Enlightenment would win over Europe.

Johann Friedrich Struensee

1737-1772

Personal Background

Early life. Johann Friedrich Struensee (pronounced "stroo **en** zay") was born at Halle, a city in the German state of Saxony, on August 5, 1737. His father Adam was a Lutheran priest, who through his stern attention to the doctrine of the church was to become superintendent-general of the entire region of Schleswig and Holstein. Friedrich, therefore, was raised in a very strict and religious household. In spite of the family's rigid religious practices, Struensee grew to be a fun-loving young man. He developed a charming personality and elegant manners that gained him favor among the fashionable circles of the area. Eventually he would throw off his father's religion entirely and for a time become an atheist, or at least a skeptic about religion. In later life, he would find religious satisfaction as a deist, one who believes in God but not in organized religion.

Struensee was very bright, received a good education, and advanced rapidly. By the time he was nineteen years old, he had earned a degree as a doctor and had begun practice in the German city of Altona (now part of Hamburg, Germany). But Struensee was politically ambitious even at this young age. He announced to his friends that if he could just get a position in Copenhagen (then the capital of Norway, Denmark, and Holstein), he would make a great name for himself.

▲ **Johann Friedrich Struensee**

Event: Reforming the kingdom of Denmark.

Role: At a time that the combined kingdoms of Denmark and Norway, along with the territory of Holstein, were ruled by a council of nobles and led by an indifferent and often incapable king, Struensee captured authority in Denmark and began reforms designed to bring that country into a new age as defined by the political writers of the Enlightenment—particularly by Voltaire.

Christian VII. Opportunity came in the form of the half-mad king of Denmark, Christian VII. This young ruler had grown up in even more severe conditions than Struensee. As a child he had been regularly beaten by his tutor and had withdrawn to the company of the stable lackeys of his father's court. His father, Frederick, had been an alcoholic, and Christian, even as a child, had also become addicted.

It was a matter of great concern in Denmark when Christian, who had not long been married to Caroline Matilda, decided to make a state trip to England and France. Christian was in his early twenties and was already showing signs of insanity. He needed almost constant medical care.

As the king passed through Altona, it was suggested that he see Struensee. Apparently from the first their doctor-patient relationship was good, for Struensee was soon appointed to be Christian's traveling doctor. It was the opportunity Struensee had been waiting for. He accompanied the king on his visit to England and managed to keep the mad ruler calm and dignified. That accomplishment made him popular with both the king and the Danish people who accompanied him. By the time the entourage returned to Copenhagen, Struensee was an established member of the court.

Participation:
Reforming the Kingdom of Denmark

Enlightenment. The great writers of the Enlightenment—Voltaire and Rousseau, particularly—were just beginning to make their voices heard across Europe. Struensee had become aware of their views on politics and was anxious to become part of the reform movement. Germany was at that time a cluster of loosely united states, each ruled by its own nobleman. Denmark was so closely related to Germany that German became the language of the aristocracy there. Denmark, too, was ruled by nobles.

After a revolution in the late seventeenth century, Denmark and Norway had been ruled by a king and a council made up of landowners. The peasants there were mostly farmers who rented small strips of land from the nobles and paid the rent partly from their produce and partly by working on larger sections held independently by each nobleman. Under Danish law, these peasants were forbidden to leave the land they had rented. In fact, their sons inherited the right to rent the same land, thus assuring the noblemen's continued control over the land and the peasants who worked it.

But Denmark had begun to find its way among the nations of the world. It had allied itself to Russia. The security of this alliance allowed trade to flourish, and Danish shipping and naval power grew. There was even some attempt to establish factories in Denmark. What better place for a young revolutionary to begin reforms than in an old-fashioned aristocratic state where some industrial reform had already started? Struensee began to establish himself as a necessary support for Christian.

This task was made easier by a rift between Christian and his young wife, Caroline Matilda. The sheltered sister of King George III of England, she had been married to Christian when she was fifteen years old. Christian was fond of his wife for a short time but then began to chase other women and to drink even more heavily. Caroline Matilda had no training that would help her adjust to this situation, especially in a strange country. In a short time, the two were separated, although living in the same great castle. Struensee saw this division as an opportunity. He would bring the king and queen together again and then use the naive queen to achieve his goals in government. His first goal was to be the absolute ruler of Denmark-Norway.

Except for one problem, Struensee's plan worked very well. With the queen's help, he became a secretary in the court and persuaded the king to give him a title. He became Count Struensee. In 1771, he became the equivalent of prime minister, again with Caroline Matilda's help. The two accomplished this merely by finding the right moment of weakness during which to present the king with a paper to sign announcing the appointment. They used the same technique to get the king's signature on a paper that gave Struensee all the king's powers. Under the new edict, no law could be enacted or enforced unless an order had been signed by Struensee. The king was then pushed aside. Struensee and Caroline Matilda were in charge of Denmark-Norway.

Idealist and activist. Struensee was still fairly young, impulsive, and idealistic. He was also very self-confident and not about to wait for anyone to agree with his half-baked plan. First he abolished the council of nobles, fired the minister of foreign affairs, and became absolute dictator. Then within little more than a year, he enacted more than six hundred reforms. He established hospitals for orphans, reduced government staffs, raised the pay of officials so that they would no longer need to raise money by selling government favors, and freed industry and trade from government control. He relaxed, but did not completely eliminate, rules that held serfs in bondage to nobles. Struensee also began to reform criminal laws. A serf could no longer be put to death for theft, for example.

Struensee believed that having two languages, German and Danish, in the country was harmful and would hinder the success of his reforms. He declared that the language of the country would be German, even though some citizens resented the action. Struensee also drew resentment from the old nobles and ministers from whom he neglected to seek support. But his greatest mistake was entering a romantic relationship with the queen.

At first Struensee had planned only to use Caroline Matilda as a tool for his own ambitions, but the two became intimate as they conspired for power. Struensee spent much of the government money he had saved in his reforms entertaining Caroline Matilda with elaborate banquets and dances. While he was rising to power, he had lived in a dark and small apartment in a remote part of the palace. Now he moved to an apartment a floor above the queen's rooms and had a secret stairway built between them. Rumors spread about their relationship.

Before Struensee had come to Denmark, the king had not been popular among his subjects, being the object of mockery. He was much shorter than even Caroline Matilda, and she was not a tall woman. Christian liked to go off with his stable friends in search of women, and he often returned to the palace in the early morning so drunk that he had to be picked up out of the gutters. The citizens of Copenhagen sometimes threw stones at their drunken king. Struensee seemed a better alternative. Then, too, most of the citizens liked what he seemed to be trying to do. But with rumors flying, he began to lose popularity. One rumor had it that the king was being held prisoner in his own palace. Juliana, Christian's stepmother, and her son Frederick took advantage of these rumors to fuel hostility toward Struensee, the man who had defiled Caroline Matilda, the idol of Denmark. Other nobles, fearing his reforms, turned against him as well.

Failed mission. Whether personal ambition or idealism were Struensee's goals, he never survived to see them through. On January 17, 1772, a group of ex-ministers and nobles marshaled by Juliana used Struensee's own tactics against him. They persuaded the king to sign an order for his arrest. The reform minister was tried for treason and for adultry with the queen. He was sentenced to death.

Aftermath

Execution. On April 28, 1772, Struensee and one of his cronies were beheaded. Caroline Matilda was also arrested, but at the last moment, brother George III stepped in to rescue her. She was sent to a castle in Germany, where she died four years later.

Juliana and Frederick. Juliana became the real ruler of Denmark for a short time and threw out many of Struensee's reforms. Later Ové Hough-Guldberg, who had been an ally of Juliana, became the prime minister. Governing Denmark under the advisement of the council of nobles, he reinstalled some of the laws that kept the serfs at the total will of the nobles.

Frederick matured and became ruler of Denmark for fifty-five years. Ironically, it was Frederick who succeeded in making the land reforms started by Struensee. Under Frederick Denmark became prosperous, mostly due to the reforms started by one of the most loved and hated rulers in Danish history—Struensee.

For More Information

Chapman, Hester W. *Caroline Matilda: Queen of Denmark.* New York: Coward, McCann and Geoghegan, 1971.

Lauring, Palle. *A History of the Kingdom of Denmark,* 2nd ed. Translated by David Hohnen. Copenhagen: Host and Son, 1960.

Oakley, Stewart. *A Short History of Denmark.* New York: Praeger, 1972.

Georges Danton

1759-1794

Personal Background

Early life. Georges-Jacques Danton was born in 1759, in the French town of Arcis-sur-Aube. His father was a lawyer and a minor government official in Arcis; his mother, his father's second wife, came from a middle-class background of craftsmen. The Dantons themselves were a middle-class but prominent family in Arcis, living in a large house facing the public square in the heart of that small town. When Georges was two years old, his father died, leaving his mother to look after Georges and his three sisters. It is known that one of his sisters eventually married and another became a nun, but virtually nothing else is known about his siblings.

While Georges was in grade school, he showed no interest in either history or mathematics but excelled in Latin. Because of this, his family decided to push him in the direction of the priesthood, and Georges was sent to a seminary-prep school in Troyes. Within a few years, however, it was clear to the family that Georges' interests lay elsewhere, and at the age of fourteen he was transferred to a high school run by priests, but not connected with a monastery.

Danton was at the school for only two years, but he made a substantial impression on his classmates. By this time, he had grown into a giant—tall, big-boned, and heavyset, with a face

▲ Georges Danton

Event: Inciting the French Revolution.

Role: An early leader of the French Revolution, Georges Danton incited the French people to rebel against the monarchy of Louis XVI. He helped organize the first stages of the revolution, including the storming of the Bastille and, later, the execution of the king.

scarred by smallpox that made him difficult to forget. This, combined with his loud voice and sweeping gestures, made him an imposing presence wherever he went. He was also known to be compulsive and determined, and a remarkable speaker; when he was sixteen, he intervened on behalf of a classmate who was about to be slapped with a ruler for punishment. His teacher was furious with Danton, but the school's principal found his argument against corporal punishment so convincing that he forbade it.

That same year, the new king of France was being crowned in the cathedral at Rheims, and the students were told to write an essay on the subject. The day after the assignment was given, Danton cut class and went to Rheims on foot—a seventy-mile walk. Although his essay was a brilliant firsthand account of the subject, he was almost expelled for the prank. Later, he told his classmates that he'd just wanted to see how they made a king and that it was worth the effort.

Young urban professional. In 1780, when Danton was twenty-one, he moved to Paris to pursue a career in law. His brash attitude (highly prized by many in the legal profession) quickly got him an apprenticeship from a lawyer named Vinot. It was a low-level job, but it put Danton in contact with every prominent lawyer in Paris. In his free time, Danton studied law on his own, knowing that he would eventually take the bar. He also began to frequent a nearby café, the Café de l'Ecole, a hangout for students and young lawyers. Danton soon became friendly with the owner and his family—especially the owner's daughter, Antoinette Charpentier, whom he married.

Danton formally entered the legal profession in 1785. For the next two years, he practiced law in Paris and saved money in order to buy a prestigious government post in the court of the king's council. It was a prestigious and expensive undertaking, but in March 1787 he was able to buy the position. This was Danton's entrance into politics.

An obsolete regime. Meanwhile, the government of Louis XVI was entering a state of political crisis. A decade earlier, out of hatred for the English, it had begun financing the American Revolution. It did this by obtaining enormous loans, which soon put

▲ The storming of the Bastille, July 14, 1789; within a month, deputies of the nobility voted away virtually all of the privileges they had been historically granted, ending the feudal regime forever.

the country in debt. By 1780 the French economy had fallen into a recession, and the wages of most of its citizens dropped, along with the king's revenue. By 1781 one-half of the country's expenditures went toward paying off the national debt. Although Louis XVI had little interest in politics, he must have realized that a crisis was at hand; he hired a series of finance ministers to take care of the problem for him. In 1786 the finance minister Charles de Calonne announced the bad news: France was bankrupt. Worse yet, he concluded that no hope for recovery was possible without a complete reform of the tax structure. Given the situation, any reform inevitably meant imposing taxes on the nobility, a move that would surely be resisted by that politically powerful class.

Calonne urged Louis XVI to convene a special meeting of representatives for the nobility, the Assembly of Notables. Calonne hoped to convince the assembly to approve his program, but when they met in February 1787 his hopes were crushed. The assembly overwhelmingly voted against any change in the status quo.

Louis XVI then took the matter to the Parliament of Paris, hoping that it would approve the plan. But the parliament reacted the same way as the Assembly of Notables had and, to evade the issue, it argued that the proposed tax could only be approved by the Estates General, an advisory body representing the three social classes of France: the clergy (130,000 French citizens); the nobility (400,000); and everyone else (the Third Estate—26,000,000 or 98 percent of the people). On May 4, 1789, the Estates General convened at Versailles to attack the economic crisis. Meanwhile, the political scene in Paris was exploding.

Participation: Inciting the French Revolution

The Cordeliers district. The convention of the Estates General required elections, and Paris was divided into sixty districts for the purpose of electing deputies as Parisian representatives of the Third Estate. Still, only male land-owners who paid a fee were eligible to vote. Danton was living in the Cordeliers district, and as the owner of some land in his hometown of Arcis, was eligible.

By the time the Estates General convened in Versailles, Danton was involved in a group of Cordeliers who gathered to discuss and debate the news. News of the conference in Versailles was upsetting. The Third Estate, representing the vast majority of the French population, was not getting fair treatment in the proceedings. Members of the clergy and nobility were breaking ranks, joining the Third Estate. The Third Estate ultimately proclaimed itself the National Assembly and proceeded to make its own laws. Spread by rumor, each development in Versailles caused further agitation of the populace in Paris. Eventually, riots began.

The storming of the Bastille. Danton hurried to the Church of the Cordeliers—a Franciscan monastery—and assem-

DÉCLARATION
DES DROITS DE L'HOMME
ET DU CITOYEN,

Décrétés par l'Assemblée Nationale dans les Séances des 20, 21, 23, 24 et 26 août 1789, acceptés par le Roi.

PRÉAMBULE.

Les représentans du peuple François, constitués en assemblée nationale, considérant que l'ignorance, l'oubli ou le mépris des droits de l'homme sont les seules causes des malheurs publics et de la corruption des gouvernemens, ont résolu d'exposer, dans une déclaration solemnelle, les droits naturels, inaliénables et sacrés de l'homme; afin que cette déclaration, constamment présente à tous les membres du corps social, leur rappelle sans cesse leurs droits et leurs devoirs; afin que les actes du pouvoir législatif et ceux du pouvoir exécutif, pouvant être à chaque instant comparés avec le but de toute institution politique, en soient plus respectés; afin que les réclamations des citoyens, fondées désormais sur des principes simples et incontestables, tournent toujours au maintien de la constitution et du bonheur de tous.

En conséquence, l'assemblée nationale reconnoît et déclare, en présence et sous les auspices de l'Être suprême, les droits suivans de l'homme et du citoyen.

ARTICLE PREMIER.

Les hommes naissent et demeurent libres et égaux en droits; les distinctions sociales ne peuvent être fondées que sur l'utilité commune.

ART. II.

Le but de toute association politique est la conservation des droits naturels et imprescriptibles de l'homme; ces droits sont la liberté, la propriété, la sûreté, et la résistance à l'oppression.

ART. III.

Le principe de toute souveraineté réside essentiellement dans la nation; nul corps, nul individu ne peut exercer d'autorité qui n'en émane expressément.

ART. IV.

La liberté consiste à pouvoir faire tout ce qui ne nuit pas à autrui. Ainsi, l'exercice des droits naturels de chaque homme, n'a de bornes que celles qui assurent aux autres membres de la société la jouissance de ces mêmes droits; ces bornes ne peuvent être déterminées que par la loi.

ART. V.

La loi n'a le droit de défendre que les actions nuisibles à la société. Tout ce qui n'est pas défendu par la loi ne peut être empêché, et nul ne peut être contraint à faire ce qu'elle n'ordonne pas.

ART. VI.

La loi est l'expression de la volonté générale; tous les citoyens ont droit de concourir personnellement, ou par leurs représentans, à sa formation; elle doit être la même pour tous, soit qu'elle protege, soit qu'elle punisse. Tous les citoyens étant égaux à ses yeux, sont également admissibles à toutes dignités, places et emplois publics, selon leur capacité et sans autres distinctions que celles de leurs vertus et de leurs talens.

ART. VII.

Nul homme ne peut être accusé, arrêté, ni détenu que dans les cas déterminés par la loi, et selon les formes qu'elle a prescrites. Ceux qui sollicitent, expédient, exécutent ou font exécuter des ordres arbitraires, doivent être punis; mais tout citoyen appelé ou saisi en vertu de la loi, doit obéir à l'instant; il se rend coupable par la résistance.

ART. VIII.

La loi ne doit établir que des peines strictement et évidemment nécessaires, et nul ne peut être puni qu'en vertu d'une loi établie et promulguée antérieurement au délit, et légalement appliquée.

ART. IX.

Tout homme étant présumé innocent jusqu'à ce qu'il ait été déclaré coupable, s'il est jugé indispensable de l'arrêter, toute rigueur qui ne seroit pas nécessaire pour s'assurer de sa personne doit être sévèrement réprimée par la loi.

ART. X.

Nul ne doit être inquiété pour ses opinions, mêmes religieuses, pourvu que leur manifestation ne trouble pas l'ordre public établi par la loi.

ART. XI.

La libre communication des pensées et des opinions est un des droits les plus précieux de l'homme: tout citoyen peut donc parler, écrire, imprimer librement: sauf à répondre de l'abus de cette liberté dans les cas déterminés par la loi.

ART. XII.

La garantie des droits de l'homme et du citoyen nécessite une force publique: cette force est donc instituée pour l'avantage de tous, et non pour l'utilité particuliere de ceux à qui elle est confiée.

ART. XIII.

Pour l'entretien de la force publique, et pour les dépenses d'administration, une contribution commune est indispensable: elle doit être également répartie entre tous les citoyens, en raison de leurs facultés.

ART. XIV.

Les citoyens ont le droit de constater par eux-mêmes ou par leurs représentans, la nécessité de la contribution publique, de la consentir librement, d'en suivre l'emploi, et d'en déterminer la quotité, l'assiette, le recouvrement et la durée.

ART. XV.

La société a le droit de demander compte à tout agent public de son administration.

ART. XVI.

Toute société, dans laquelle la garantie des droits n'est pas assurée, ni la séparation des pouvoirs déterminée, n'a point de constitution.

ART. XVII.

Les propriétés étant un droit inviolable et sacré, nul ne peut en être privé, si ce n'est lorsque la nécessité publique, légalement constatée l'exige évidemment, et sous la condition d'une juste et préalable indemnité.

Se vend à Paris, chez Gouion, marchand de musique, grand'cour du Palais-royal où se trouve le Tableau de la Constitution faisant pendant à celui-ci.

▲ "The Declaration of the Rights of Man," a new constitution prompted by the revolutionary situation, was signed by Louis XVI himself.

bled a citizens' militia. Playing off the people's fear that the king would send German and Swiss mercenary troops to subdue Paris, Danton's speech drew over five hundred volunteers. But when Danton was bluntly informed that there were no mercenary troops descending on Paris, he continued to urge opposition to the king and proclaimed that the monarchy was finished.

For arms, the Bataillon des Cordeliers and other groups went to the Bastille, the fortress prison of Paris, which was more a symbol of monarchic power than a source of weapons. On July 14, 1789, a day still commemorated by the French, the Bastille was stormed and taken by the mobs. This act had great impact upon the proceedings in Versailles: within a month, deputies of the nobility voted away virtually all of the privileges they had been historically granted, ending the feudal regime forever. "The Declaration of the Rights of Man," a new constitution prompted by the revolutionary situation, was signed by Louis XVI himself. He did this under pressure, though, knowing that his refusal to do so would end his reign.

Because of Danton's role in the storming of the Bastille, he was elected president of the Cordeliers district. And although Paris contained sixty districts in all, Danton's firm leadership and relentless participation soon made him a powerful force in the city's government activities. At his insistence, the district published a manifesto that was posted all over Paris, urging the people of the city to march on Versailles with his Bataillon des Cordeliers. Danton himself stayed in Paris. On October 7th, news reached Danton that the Chateau of Versailles had been stormed by the mob, and that the royal family was returning to Paris for protection.

The pamphleteers. Among other freedoms, the "Declaration of the Rights of Man" guaranteed a free press, and upon its enactment Paris was flooded with political pamphlets. The most famous of the pamphleteers were Jean-Paul Marat and Camille Desmoulins. Desmoulins was Danton's good friend and reported on all of Danton's achievements in his weekly pamphlet. This only increased Danton's popularity, and he was reelected president of his district four times in a row.

The Paris Commune. In January 1790 the Cordeliers district nominated Danton as its representative to the Paris Commune, a city council headed by the mayor of Paris. Unfortunately, Danton's past agitations made him a controversial figure in the eyes of most of the commune's members, and his dual role (he was still president of his district) frequently put him in uncomfortable positions. The National Assembly, however, solved that problem for him. Fearing Danton's growing power, the assembly dissolved the sixty districts of Paris and reorganized them into forty-eight voting blocs; they also made it illegal to hold meetings except at election time.

Danton immediately sought out another position of power, at the exclusive Club of the Jacobins. Although a powerful political group, the Jacobins were not organized around a district and therefore survived the new law. Their new president, Robespierre, was suddenly a very powerful man himself; Danton hoped that by joining the Jacobins, he could remain an influential figure. The Jacobins, however, were an elite organization and were not enamored with Danton's fiery rhetoric. Having lost his district and having been rejected by the Paris Commune and the Jacobins, Danton founded his own club—the Club of the Cordeliers.

The Club of the Cordeliers. With Desmoulins' help, Danton was able to get a charter for his club, officially called the Society of the Friends of the Rights of Man. The club's slogan, "Liberté, Egalité, Fraternité," was created by Danton and has since become the national motto of the French Republic. His activities became increasingly revolutionary, and he was removed from the Paris Commune in September 1790. It didn't seem to matter however; Danton's real influence had always been over the people of Paris.

The following year, Louis XVI planned an Easter vacation away from Paris and arranged to have the National Guard protect him and his family as they left. One of the battalions given this task was the former Bataillon des Cordeliers, whose members were still loyal to Danton. Danton was notified of the trip in advance, and he effectively prevented the king's departure by inciting demonstrations outside the palace, the Tuileries. Even factions of the National Guard turned on the monarch, for regardless of the king's intentions, his trip was perceived as an escape.

With Danton heading the Cordeliers, and with the pamphlets of Desmoulins and Marat in support, the rebellion instigated by these three men suddenly became a movement to abolish the monarchy altogether. The Cordeliers drew up a petition, demanding that the king be regarded as having abdicated his throne by his attempted flight. On July 17 it was taken to the Champ de Mars, where the people of Paris were called to sign it. The mayor of Paris disapproved of the purpose of this "unlawful" assembly and called in troops of the National Guard to disperse the crowd. A fight broke out and several people were killed in the incident, known as the massacre of the Champ de Mars.

Afterward, the government clamped down on anti-royalists, and Danton fled to England for six weeks. When he returned to Paris, he was elected deputy public prosecutor for the Paris Commune. For a while, it appeared that Danton had lost his revolutionary zeal and was prepared to accept a peaceful role in the public service. This appearance proved to be false.

The end of French monarchy. Danton and others arranged to attack the royal palace on August 10, 1792, to end the monarchy forever and establish a republic. Many factions conspired together in this widely known event. Louis XVI, who had been warned, took his family to the nearby riding school, where the National Assembly had been meeting since the king's return to Paris. Members of the assembly put them safely in the newspaper reporters' gallery. When the revolutionaries arrived at the Tuileries, they overpowered the king's Swiss guards and took over. The mob killed the guards and servants, and ransacked the palace. At the same time, representatives of the different quarters of Paris took over City Hall. They sent messengers to the assembly, demanding that the king be dethroned. The assembly did not do this immediately but instead suspended his power and placed him under guard. A new ministry was formed and Danton, the most conspicuous leader of the insurrection, was made a minister of justice.

Three days later, a decree was passed that summoned a national convention to draft a new constitution. Even though most of France was still loyal to the king, the circumstances mandated that the new constitution abolish the monarchy for a republic.

Year One. The convention met on September 21 and immediately proclaimed France a republic. The next day was declared the first day of Year One of French liberty. The more radical Parisians immediately took the law into their own hands, arresting three thousand citizens they accused of conspiring with foreign nobles to bring back the monarchy. For two days in September, hundreds of suspected traitors were summarily executed. The extremists in the convention wanted the king executed as well, for it was widely believed that he secretly encouraged foreign countries to invade France and reestablish his reign. They put the matter to a vote and won by a narrow margin. Louis was executed on January 21, 1793.

By August 1792 Prussia invaded France. French troops fought them back well beyond the border, invading Germany until the entire country was taken. The convention issued proclamations calling on all freedom-loving peoples of Europe to revolt against their monarchies. This bold statement frightened every nation in Europe—England was especially concerned about French expansionist aims. On February 1 the convention declared war on England and Holland, who formed a coalition against France; later that year, when Spain and the Holy Roman Empire joined the effort, France was at war with all of its neighbors. In March, the Dutch drove the French out of Holland. This military loss convinced the convention that they could not create a new, permanent government and fight a war at the same time. The decision was made, then, to give practically unlimited powers to an interim government composed of nine people—the Committee of Public Safety. The following day, on April 7, 1793, Danton became a member of the committee.

For the following three months, Danton was effectively the head of the French government. His main concern was the turbulent state of foreign affairs; he wanted an end to the hostilities and tried in vain to negotiate a compromise with France's enemies.

Fashion During the Revolution

Despite the fact that almost every major figure in the revolution was eventually guillotined, most French citizens were unconcerned with politics and therefore free from danger. For them, the executions were a public spectacle—a soap opera—and fun to watch. It even became fashionable for ladies to wear jewelry in the shape of miniature guillotines—a symbol of progress.

The wars, he felt, were draining the citizens' income through increased taxes and creating a class of traitors who were becoming rich from the spoils of war. In pursuing peace, however, he was beginning to be regarded as a moderate. When his first term in the committee expired on July 10, the convention did not reelect him.

Disagreement in France

Not all of France endorsed the frenzied activities in Paris; in Brittany, on the north coast, the citizens were still loyal to the king and refused to fight for the republic that had killed him. One by one, other large cities revolted against the revolution: Marseille, Bordeaux, Lyons, and the southern port of Toulon, which welcomed English invaders as their allies. With swift efficiency, the Committee of Public Safety repelled the foreign invasions and turned its attention to the rebellious cities. Lyons was bombarded and captured, and two thousand of its citizens were massacred as a lesson to other cities. Even though the insurrection was finally put down, it demonstrated how widespread hatred of the new republic had become.

Reign of terror. The committee viewed anyone with "counter-revolutionary" sentiments as enemies. From September 1793 to July 1794, a Reign of Terror descended upon France, as more and more suspects went to the guillotine for real or imagined offenses.

Danton, while officially out of the government, continued to speak as the voice of the people, urging moderation. He and Desmoulins both felt that the violence had gone too far. In December 1793, he bluntly told the radical revolutionaries that their role was over. This angered both Jacobins and the Committee of Public Safety. Robespierre, who had risen to become the most powerful member of the committee, had both Danton and Desmoulins arrested on the night of March 29, 1794.

At his public trial, Danton tried to rally the spectators around him, condemning the Revolutionary Tribunal he faced. Instead of testifying in his own defense, he started giving another of his fiery speeches on the excesses of the revolution. His effectiveness on the audience was so feared that he was silenced by a new law, created on the spot, that forbade testimony by a suspect who insulted the justice system. He and all his friends were convicted and executed together on April 5.

Aftermath

Robespierre. After the execution of Robespierre's most influential opponents, he became a dictator in essence. Members of the convention were intimidated by him, fearing that even the slightest dissent could result in their executions as well. Eventually they conspired to have him arrested. On July 29, 1794, as he began to speak to the convention, its members cried, "Down with the tyrant!" For a moment, he could not speak, and a deputy shouted, "The blood of Danton chokes him!" Robespierre was sent to the guillotine.

After Robespierre's execution, the mood in France changed considerably. People were getting tired of the constant political upheavals and the endless bloodshed of the Reign of Terror. The principles of the revolution had gotten lost in the struggles for power at home and abroad. Many felt that life had been so much simpler when France was a monarchy. And although the age of kings was clearly gone, France would soon experience another sort of all-powerful leader; within five years, the dictator Napoléon Bonaparte would be its unquestioned ruler.

Danton's Last Words

As the last to be guillotined, Danton said these words to his executioner: "Show my head to the people.... It's worth the trouble."

For More Information

Christophe, Robert. *Danton.* New York: Doubleday, 1967.

Rude, George. *Revolutionary Europe, 1783-1815.* New York: Harper and Row, 1964.

Taylor, A. J. P. *Revolutions and Revolutionaries.* New York: Atheneum, 1980.

Maria Carolina

1752-1814

Personal Background

The family of Maria Theresa. Maria Carolina was born at Vienna in 1752, the daughter of Francis I, emperor of Germany. Her mother, Maria Theresa (1717-1780), queen of Hungary and Bohemia and archduchess of Austria, was a powerful ruler over much of Europe. While bearing and raising sixteen children, she initiated a great number of reforms designed to help the poor of her kingdoms improve their lives. Raising and educating her children occupied an equal place with reforming Austria and Hungary and defending her empire against the Prussian ruler, Frederick.

Maria Carolina was the fifth of Theresa's daughters who survived infancy—all with Christian names that included Maria or Marie. There were in the family Marie Amélie, Marie Anne, Maria Christina, Marie Elizabeth, Maria Carolina—and later, the most famous of the sisters, Marie-Antoinette (born Maria Antonia). All were raised to become queens, a role that demanded training in entertaining and ornamenting a palace, but not necessarily learning about reading, writing, history, or other subjects taught to the boys of the family. (It was said of Maria Antonia that upon marrying the future king of France, she was so poorly educated that she could not properly spell her own name.)

Early life. Carolina's father was not much of a ruler. He had grown up in a section under French influence and spoke French,

▲ Maria Carolina

Event: Resisting the influences of the French Revolution.

Role: Maria Carolina, on becoming queen of Naples, initiated great reforms to ease the tyranny of nobles and provide aid and education for the poor. The French Revolution, however, brought unrest to Naples. The dissension among citizens who had previously admired her along with the French Revolutionists' execution of her favorite sister, Marie-Antoinette, changed Maria Carolina into a tyrannical ruler who resisted French invasions of Naples for many years.

even though he ruled a region where German was the language. He preferred hunting and drinking to ruling, so Maria Theresa was the real manager of all the land the two ruled. For much of the time, therefore, the training of the girls was left to strong women tutors. Otherwise, as was the woman's role in those days, the girls were protected within the palace and sheltered from worldly affairs. Carolina was born into this rather dull and lonely station.

Carolina's life changed, however, at age three, when her mother gave birth to another girl, Maria Antonia. Carolina became an almost constant companion to her younger sister and the two came to be great friends. Playing always with a younger sister only added to Carolina's immaturity. Finally, when Carolina was about eleven and Antonia eight, they were separated and placed under the care of two different nursemaids. By that time, Maria Theresa had already arranged marriages for both of them. Maria Antonia would, as soon as she was of age, marry the crown prince of France; Maria Carolina would marry Ferdinand IV, king of Naples.

Marriage. When she was fifteen, therefore, Carolina left the palace at Vienna to travel to Caserta, near Naples, for her wedding. A few years later, Antonia, then with her name changed to the French Antoinette, would leave home to wed in Paris. Both girls were uncommonly beautiful—a bright addition to any court. But there, the parallels between the two would fade. While Marie-Antoinette concerned herself with entertaining and beautifying the court with her presence, Carolina took take active part in ruling her kingdom—much as her mother had done, and for the same reasons.

Ferdinand IV, king of Naples, was not much concerned with ruling. Like many of the noblemen of his day, he preferred to hunt, ride, drink, and chase women rather than to attend to the

Carolina and Antoinette

"For this princess [Carolina] really possessed a masculine understanding, with great natural and acquired powers of mind, scarcely inferior to those enjoyed by the profoundest statesman. She had a cool head in council, was capable of forming a just conception of things in general, and had acquired a knowledge of men and manners far exceeding that of her unfortunate sister ... who, though she had a greater portion of the milk of human kindness ... than Carolina, possessed a capacity by no means capable of executing any plan that required firmness or perseverance." (Bearne, p. 64) duties of a ruler. Carolina left for her wedding with misgivings. She had never seen her future husband and did not know whether she would be treated with kindness or cruelty. The first meetings were not encouraging but not so bad either:

> He is very ugly but one gets used to that; and as to his character, it is all much better than I was told.... What irritates me most is that he thinks he is handsome and clever, and he is neither the one nor the other. I must tell you and confess that I don't love him except from duty. (From a letter to her nursemaid, Frau von Lerchenfeld, quoted in Bearne, p. 71)

Von Lerchenfeld had taught her well, however, and Carolina was determined to become more than an ornament at court. She courted her husband and treated him so kindly that soon he was quite willing to leave most of the ruling to her. Carolina followed in her mother's path. She initiated reforms to help the poor, reduce the power of the nobles, and expand opportunities for education. Along the way, she angered the nobles and some of the elite who resented the changes in educational opportunities. Carolina made a few more enemies when she persuaded her husband to fire his prime minister and replace him with one of her own choosing—John Acton, a sea commander who could build a navy to combat the plague of Barbary coast pirates attacking Naples' shipping. But mostly she ruled so kindly and made such wise changes that her subjects in the two Naples (the area around present-day Naples and the island of Sicily) adored her. For twenty-two years, from 1768 to 1790, Carolina ruled a peaceful, and for the most part, happy kingdom. But then events in France began to be strongly felt in Naples.

Participation: Resisting the Influences of the French Revolution

Amélia and the future king of France. Again following the path of her mother, Carolina had borne a child nearly every year of her marriage and had spent much of her time arranging suitable marriages for them with other royal families (although most of the

royal families of Europe were related to each other). She had kept in touch with Marie-Antoinette and, when Marie-Antoinette's first son was born, the two mothers agreed that this crown prince of France would marry Carolina's daughter, Amélia. But this arrangement was delayed when revolution erupted in France.

France. The Enlightenment had brought new ideas to France, and it was not at all odd that a new view of government should spring up in that country. The noble families there lived in great wealth and luxury, while on the whole the people of France were among the poorest in Europe. The country was a fertile place for the growth of the ideas of freedom and individual worth taught by such writers as Voltaire and Jean-Jacques Rousseau. In 1789 unhappy French people rose up in rebellion against King Louis XVI, the husband of Marie-Antoinette.

Problems had arisen long before that. In 1774 Louis had inherited a country steeped in poverty and discontent. He had the intelligence to employ good ambassadors to begin reforms, but he had

> ## Carolina's Success
>
> The success of Carolina in arranging marriages for her children is illustrated by the titles held by her daughters. They became the Empress of Germany, the Queen of France, the Grand-Duchess of Tuscany, the Princess of Asturias, and the Queen of Sardinia.

been persuaded by people at court (one of whom was his wife) to delay many reform movements. By 1777 the French government was nearly bankrupt. Conditions failed to improve over the following ten years as Louis proved incapable of making important decisions. On July 11, 1789, a peasant mob, mostly women, converged on the palace demanding reform. The king's family was moved from Versailles to Paris. A bloody revolution, directed by disorganized leaders, had begun.

Change in Naples. Carolina feared that the turmoil that was beginning in France would spill over into her own kingdom. Already she sensed some unhappiness in the people of Naples. But now the queen of France had been placed under virtual arrest in the Tuileries (she would soon be moved to the Temple

◄
Castel Nuovo in Naples; Carolina feared that the turmoil that was beginning in France would spill over into her own kingdom.

▲ Marie-Antoinette, Maria Carolina's favorite sister; after the French Revolutionists executed Marie-Antoinette, Maria Carolina changed into a tyrannical ruler who resisted French invasions of Naples for many years.

in Paris and then to a real prison). Carolina came to both fear and hate the French who had so mistreated her sister. She ordered Acton, Naples' prime minister, to improve both the navy and army in preparation for an attempted invasion from France.

Carolina had reason to worry. Once when French warships put in to Naples harbor and requested supplies and permission to land a new French ambassador, she had at first refused. But under threat of French bombardment of the city, she relented. The French had responded by giving lessons in rebellion to sympathizers in Naples. When they finally left, thousands of Naples citizens gathered to see them off. The new ambassador, who was found to be spreading subversion, was asked to leave but refused.

Carolina responded to all this by completely changing her style of government. She was no longer primarily worried about the well-being of the peasants, nor was she interested in making more reforms. Instead, she concentrated on strengthening the army and navy. To protect against rebellion within Naples she organized a secret police, a group who met with her secretly to report on actions in the city. The citizens of Naples were intimidated into submission as corps of the secret police made nightly raids on suspected rebels. Those arrested found themselves in prison, and those outside often did not hear of them again.

The death of Marie-Antoinette. Almost all Carolina's relatives were kings, queens, dukes, emperors, or duchesses in the large and small nations of Europe. Carolina began to actively encourage these relatives to join her in opposing the French and in attempting to free her sister, Marie-Antoinette. But most of the rulers lived in fear of a France that seemed to have gone wild. In January 1793 King Louis XVI was executed, having been convicted of treason in a French court. In October of that year, Marie-Antoinette, too, was guillotined, after more than a year of imprisonment.

War. The danger was now conspicuous. Carolina had organized an army of forty-five thousand men and a fleet of forty fine ships. To this she was now able to add assistance from England. Through her good friend Lady Wellington, the wife of a British military leader, she persuaded Lord Nelson, commodore of the British navy, to join her in fighting the French fleet. Meanwhile, a young general from Corsica began to lead great victories for the French in Spain. Soon General Napoléon Bonaparte would take advantage of the confusion in the French government to take complete control of the country. Under him, the might of France grew. The army and navy of Naples were no longer an obstacle to Bonaparte's army.

A French conquest. France invaded Naples in 1808 and set up a new kingdom there, and Carolina and Ferdinand escaped to Palermo in Sicily. The pressure on Ferdinand had been too great. Now he began to blame all the troubles of Naples on Carolina's anger at the French. For a short time, the king and queen separated, and she went to live with relatives in Austria. But then, the forces of Naples and England regrouped and forced the French to agree to a peace treaty. Naples was returned to Ferdinand, who took active control of the nation. If the last years of his wife's rule had been filled with horror and intrigue, they paled in comparison to the treatment the peasants of Naples received from the king.

The French Revolution and her actions to suppress it had cost Carolina her authority to rule, and she had gained little. The French remained a threat to her husband, and her favorite sister was dead.

Aftermath

The war with Napoléon. With Napoléon at the helm, France now prepared to take over much of Europe. In 1808 Napoléon's forces overran Naples. It was the last blow for Carolina; the navy she had so diligently built was burned in Naples harbor to prevent it from falling to the French. It would eventually require all the strength of the British navy and a combined army of Austria and its allies to defeat the French dictator.

Carolina. After the second fall of Naples, Carolina returned to the family home in Vienna. Her health began to fail and she suffered several strokes. One of these finally proved fatal, and she died September 7, 1814. Carolina did not live to see the French governor of Naples die and her sons and husband return to take control of the city.

Ferdinand's rule now had no calming influence. "After the death of the Queen, Ferdinand was a far worse man and a more cruel and tyrannical ruler than he had ever been during the life and influence of the sister of Marie-Antoinette" (Bearne, p. 428).

The French Revolution. The revolutionaries of France were far more disorganized in their efforts than had been those of America a few years earlier. Their cruelty and lack of coordination opened the way for Napoléon to take absolute command of the country and to lead it on a costly series of wars of acquisition. Upon his final defeat, France once again returned to the monarchy its people had once so violently protested. It would be many years before France would return to a more democratic form of government.

For More Information

Bearne, Mrs. *A Sister of Marie-Antoinette: The Life-Story of Maria Carolina, Queen of Naples.* London: T. Fisher Unwin, 1907.

Hearsey, John. *Marie-Antoinette.* New York: E. P. Dutton, 1973.

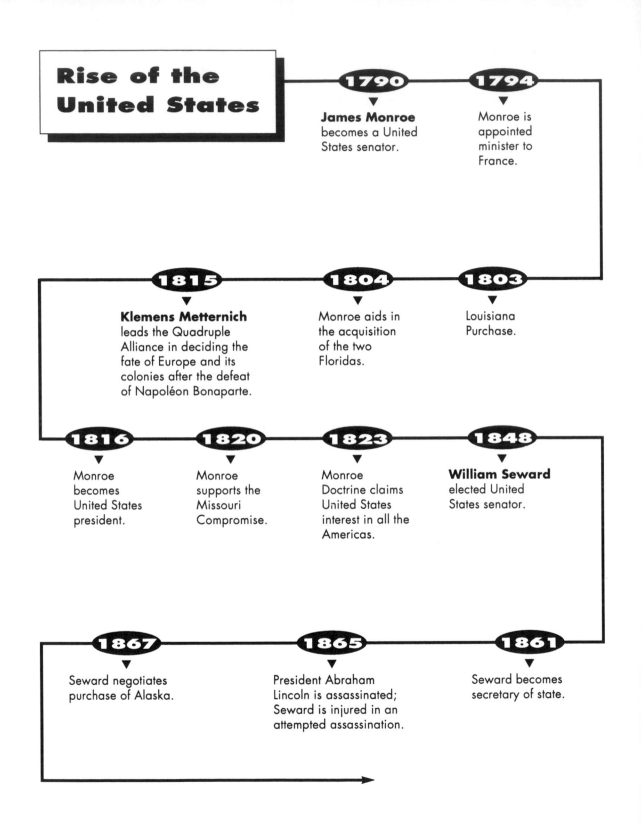

Rise of the United States

1790
James Monroe becomes a United States senator.

1794
Monroe is appointed minister to France.

1815
Klemens Metternich leads the Quadruple Alliance in deciding the fate of Europe and its colonies after the defeat of Napoléon Bonaparte.

1804
Monroe aids in the acquisition of the two Floridas.

1803
Louisiana Purchase.

1816
Monroe becomes United States president.

1820
Monroe supports the Missouri Compromise.

1823
Monroe Doctrine claims United States interest in all the Americas.

1848
William Seward elected United States senator.

1867
Seward negotiates purchase of Alaska.

1865
President Abraham Lincoln is assassinated; Seward is injured in an attempted assassination.

1861
Seward becomes secretary of state.

RISE OF THE UNITED STATES

As the French armies of Napoléon Bonaparte swept across Europe in the early nineteenth century finally to be defeated in Russia and crushed by alliances dominated by the Austrian diplomat **Klemens Metternich,** the United States and Britain were at war in America. When that War of 1812 ended in a stalemate, the United States was prepared to enter the world of global politics—particularly those politics that were involved in expansion of U.S. territory. The nation had nearly doubled its area by the purchase of the Louisiana Territory from France before the war, but Spain still held Florida and much of the territory west of the Louisiana Purchase. Oregon was still held under joint British-American occupation, while Russia held the territory now known as Alaska and had established a trading post in California.

Events in Europe were to play an important role in determining the U.S. borders and in the United States becoming a world power. Metternich oversaw the division of Europe after the defeat of Napoléon. The prince, a staunch advocate of strong monarchies, guided European powers toward his own theory of "legitimacy"—the old monarchies, he claimed, had a divine right to exist, and the right and obligation to come to the aid of any smaller monarchy threatened by republicanism (the principles of those who believe in a non-monarchical government in which power resides in a body of citizens entitled to vote). The Metternich policy soon led to the restoration of a French monarchy and its inclusion in the alliance of great European nations. France was restored under the principle of "legitimacy" in order to invade Spain and return its royal family to power. The idea of legitimacy also included the notion that the established monarchies of Europe had a right to join together to restore former colonies to the European nations that previously ruled them.

In the early nineteenth century the Spanish colonies in Latin America broke away and established independent republics. One of Metternich's suggestions was that the alliances that had defeated Napoléon should combine their powers to invade South America and restore the Spanish colonial authority. This position was offensive to U.S. president **James Monroe,** but it was also an opportunity. The United States was enjoying a newfound sense of strength, having fought the more powerful Britain to a draw ten years earlier. It was now prepared to expand its own territory beyond the Mississippi River and to take its place among the world powers. Monroe saw European obstacles in the way of that progress. For one thing, Spain still held a foothold in North America since Florida and Mexico were still under Spanish rule. In 1821 Monroe engineered the purchase of Florida.

On December 2, 1823, urged on by the British, who were by that time weary of American adventure, President James Monroe defined the United States's policy in response to Metternich's "legitimacy" idea. Announced in a speech to Congress, the policy came to be called the Monroe Doctrine. With little to back his declaration except the battleships of the British navy, Monroe asserted his country's commitment to keeping the entire Western Hemisphere free of European interference. At the same time, he aimed his policy directly at Russia, announcing that no more American lands were available for foreign colonization. It was a bold doctrine that, fortunately, was supported by Britain, even though Monroe had ignored their idea of stating the anti-legitimacy policy jointly. It was also well-timed, for European countries were occupied with their own problems. The immediate effect was that the European idea of banding together to restore South America to Spain was abandoned. But that may have had more to do with

Britain's refusal to participate than with European respect for the statements of the president of an upstart young republic.

Nevertheless, the Monroe Doctrine would guide American action into the twentieth century, and one of its chief advocates would be **William Seward,** a longtime politician who became secretary of state under President Abraham Lincoln. Seward used the ideas of the doctrine to prevent European interference in the Civil War. When the war ended he turned toward France, which had taken advantage of the Civil War in the United States to establish itself in Mexico. With the war over, and again at a time when the United States had little strength for battle, Seward used diplomacy and bluff to persuade the French to withdraw their support from the Austrian leader they had installed in Mexico. French hopes for an empire collapsed, and the Mexican republic was restored.

Turning his attention to Russian holdings in America, Seward again used diplomacy to implement the Monroe Doctrine peacefully. He suggested that the United States buy the Russian interests in the Western Hemisphere. His proposal came at an appropriate time—Russia had left the area that is now Alaska to its Russian American Company. That company, mostly interested in exploiting the riches of the sea near the Bering Strait, had mishandled the native people with little financial success. Russia was ready to get rid of the whole region without further exploration of its potential, setting the price at just over $7 million. In 1868 the United States paid for the whole land, which Senator Charles Sumner named Alaska, the native word for "mainland."

By the time Ulysses S. Grant took office as president in 1869, America's power and prestige, not to mention its territory, had grown considerably.

James Monroe

1758-1831

Personal Background

Humble beginning. James Monroe was born on April 28, 1758, on a farm in eastern Virginia. Spence Monroe, his father, had come from a long-established Virginia family. The Monroes traced their ancestry to Andrew Monroe, who came from Scotland to settle in Maryland in 1647. There Andrew had become involved in a rebellion that threatened the powerful Lord Baltimore and found it necessary to flee to Virginia. James's mother, Elizabeth Jones Monroe, was also Virginia-born. Monroe was born into a solid though not wealthy family.

The family farm on which Monroe spent his early days was located on Monroe Creek, not far from the Potomac River. In those days, there were no nearby public schools. Monroe was taught to read, write, and cipher in the private school run by the local parson, Archibald Campbell. At the age of sixteen, not an uncommonly early age in his time, Monroe entered William and Mary College in Williamsburg. By this time, he was near his full growth, reaching a height of six feet, tall for that time. Deep grayish-blue eyes and a tendency to quietly listen to all sides of a discussion before making decisions—usually wise ones—made him a striking figure among the students at the college.

A patriot. Williamsburg, the capital of Virginia, was a hotbed of American patriotism in the years just before the Ameri-

▲ James Monroe

Event: Developing United States foreign policy.

Role: A veteran legislator and diplomat whose assignments in Europe had made him well aware of political philosophies on that continent, James Monroe became U.S. president after helping to make the Louisiana Purchase. As president, he directed the trade that gained Florida for the United States, but he is best known for issuing what became known as the Monroe Doctrine, which declared opposition to European interference in the Americas.

▲ By the age of sixteen Monroe stood nearly six feet, tall for that time. His tendency to quietly listen to all sides of a discussion before making decisions made him a striking figure.

can Revolution. By 1775, the year after Monroe arrived at the college, the students were anticipating war with Britain. Monroe bought a rifle and joined the students who were openly drilling on the campus. In June of that year, he was the youngest of a band of patriots that occupied the palace of the British governor, Lord Dunmore, forcing him to flee Virginia. When full-fledged war erupted between Britain and its colonies, Monroe left school to fight. He joined the Third Virginia Infantry and soon rose to the rank of lieutenant.

Monroe led troops in battles at Harlem and White Plains, and in December 1776 was with the army of George Washington when he decided to cross the Delaware River to attack at Trenton, New Jersey. Monroe volunteered to join an advance unit that slipped across the river to hold a key road junction for the advance of the main army. In the battle that followed, Monroe was hit in the shoulder by a bullet that severed an artery. The night before, he had met a doctor and recruited him for duty with the army. That doctor treated the wound and saved Monroe's life. He recovered to become a messenger for Lord Stirling (General William Alexander) and to spend the winter of 1777-78 at Valley Forge.

Army commission and the law. In an old military tradition, the surest way to earn rank as an officer was to recruit a company or a regiment. Even though he had fought in the battle at Monmouth, Monroe was not able to advance in rank. He tried to raise a regiment for the army of Virginia but failed and resigned from military duty. Virginia governor Thomas Jefferson then suggested that Monroe might prepare to serve himself and the state by studying law. He accepted Jefferson's advice, returned to William and Mary, and began to study law under Jefferson's direction. The friendship that developed between Jefferson and Monroe was an important resource for Monroe throughout his career. He thought he was through fighting, but when the war moved to Virginia in 1780, Monroe reenlisted to lead a Virginia regiment as a full colonel.

Politics. It would not be long before Monroe was involved in politics. In 1782 he won a seat in the state legislature. He was later elected to the Governor's Council, a group whose approval the governor needed in order to act. The following year the state legislature chose Monroe to represent Virginia in the Continental Congress. He soon became a leader on congressional committees, but Congress did not accomplish a great deal.

In 1786 Monroe married eighteen-year-old Elizabeth Kortright. (The couple would have two daughters, Eliza and Maria, and would remain happily married until Elizabeth's death in 1830.) The wedding took place about the same time that Monroe was becoming upset over the inaction of Congress. In the same year, he resigned to enter private law practice. He was soon back in politics, however, being elected to the state legislature in 1787. From that day forward, he labored in politics, moving steadily toward the presidency of the United States.

Monroe served in the U.S. Senate from 1790 to 1794, working always in alliance with Thomas Jefferson and the Democratic Republicans on the side of states' rights and agrarian (farming) economic communities. Monroe believed, along with his party, that the key role of the federal government was to handle foreign affairs. He therefore opposed Federalists George Washington and Alexander Hamilton who supported a strong federal government under the control of wealthy merchants and property owners. Despite their differences, George Washington appointed Monroe as minister to France in 1794.

On his return from France, Monroe served as governor of Virginia from 1799 until 1802, when Thomas Jefferson, then president, sent him back to France as a "minister extraordinary." There he was to help the U.S. minister to France, Robert Livingston, with negotiations for the Louisiana Purchase. The United States had learned in 1801 that Spain had ceded its holdings in Louisiana to France, which was then under the rule of the aggressive and powerful Napoléon I. The territory included the Mississippi River, a vital trade route for Western settlers. Acquisition of New Orleans, in particular, seemed crucial.

Fortunately France was in a poor position to maintain control of the Louisiana territory. Haiti had recently revolted against French rule, and France was preparing for war with Great Britain. France's colonial holdings in the Americas simply presented Napoléon with too many difficulties. When Livingston met with the French minister, he was surprised by an immediate offer from France to sell the entire Louisiana area. The area extended roughly from the Mississippi River in the east to the Rocky Mountains in the west, and from the Gulf of Mexico in the south to the borders of Canada in the north. Monroe and Livingston bargained over the price, finally agreeing to pay France $15 million—or about three cents an acre—for this area that would double the size of the United States.

Monroe served as minister to Spain and then to Great Britain in 1804. He made an unsuccessful bid for the presidential nomination in 1808, and then returned to Virginia as governor in 1811. He served as secretary of state under Jefferson in 1812 and again as secretary of state (1811-17) and briefly as secretary of war (1814-15) under President James Madison.

President. In 1816 Monroe was elected president of the United States at a time that a Boston newspaper later described as the "Era of Good Feeling" (Carson, p. 176). General Andrew Jackson had won a victory in New Orleans at the end of the war, and it seemed as if statesmanship would replace partisan politics; furthermore, there was an economic boom. In spite of a brief depression that broke this boom in 1789, Monroe was reelected in 1820.

One of Monroe's most important accomplishments as president was in foreign policy. His minister to London, Richard Rush, negotiated a firm Canadian-United States boundary at the forty-ninth parallel and reached an agreement on limits of armaments in the Great Lakes, along with complete demilitarization of the entire border. The Rush-Bagot Agreement has been called "the first, and, in many ways, the most effective disarmament treaty in history" (Johnson, p. 44).

Florida. For years, Florida had been a sore spot for American policymakers. Poorly administered by Spain, it served as a sanctuary for hostile Indians, fugitive slaves, slave traders, pirates, and British agents. The United States had been trying for years to buy the region from Spain. In 1818, a year after directing the army to take Amelia Island just below the Georgia border, Monroe ordered General Andrew Jackson to put down an uprising among the Seminole Indians in Georgia. Jackson was directed to follow the Indians into Florida if necessary. Although Jackson overstepped his assignment, raising the United States flag over a Florida town and executing two Britons suspected of helping the

Indians, his action resulted in negotiations with Spain that brought Florida into the United States.

Participation:
Developing United States Foreign Policy

Events in Europe. Following the defeat of French emperor Napoléon Bonaparte in Europe, the "Quadruple Alliance" of Russia, Prussia, Austria, and England that had brought about the defeat set about restoring order in Europe. Prussia, Russia, and Austria had also joined in a "Holy Alliance" to protect their mutual interests. The most influential individual in the two alliances was Austrian prime minister **Klemens Metternich** (see entry). Under his influence, both alliances took the stance of "legitimacy," which declared the right of the old monarchies to prevail over the growing republicanism and the right of the larger monarchies to interfere in rebellions in smaller kingdoms.

> ## The Missouri Compromise
>
> Monroe's presidency was not without problems. In 1819 Missouri applied for admission to the union as a "slave state." That created a heated debate in Congress and the executive branch of government. Eventually, in an agreement known as the Missouri Compromise, it was agreed that slavery within the Louisiana Purchase (of which Missouri was a part) would be prohibited north of an east-west line defined by Missouri's northern border. Monroe, a slave-owner himself, signed the agreement allowing Maine into the union at the same time as a "free state" to keep the balance in Congress.

As Napoléon was fading and the alliances divided Europe, revolts were taking place in the South American colonies claimed by Spain. Beginning in 1810, one after another of the colonies broke away from Spain to form independent countries. By 1822 most Latin American countries had won their independence. Monroe, wary of the attitudes of the large European monarchies dominated by such men as Metternich, called for recognition of the new republics.

Monroe's suspicions were confirmed when the alliances approved the rearming of France so that it could invade Spain to overthrow the new constitutional government there and reestablish Spain as a monarchy. It followed that, under Metternich's policy of legitimacy, Spain would then be joined by the other monarchies in reclaiming Spanish holdings in Latin America. But, by this time, both Britain and the United States had commercial interests in Latin America. The thought of Spanish intervention was disturbing.

Meanwhile, the Russian government was claiming part of the Oregon territory, which was under joint British-United States administration. The Russians also set up a trading post in California.

In August 1823 British Foreign Minister George Canning proposed that Britain and the United States issue a joint declaration declaring their opposition to any European country seizing any part of the collapsing Spanish empire. The United States cabinet immediately began discussing this possibility. Certainly, the British navy would be more of a deterrent to European armies of invasion than any force the United States might raise.

Most of the cabinet, as well as former presidents Thomas Jefferson and James Madison, favored the proposal. Secretary of State John Quincy Adams, however, distrusted the British and proposed that the United States make its own statement on the matter. He doubted that the Europeans had the ability to intervene, and he did not want to see America "come in as a cock-boat in the wake of a British man-of-war" (Cresson, p. 440).

The Monroe Doctrine. Adams eventually won over Monroe. In an address to Congress on December 2, 1823, the president outlined a policy that would later come to be known as the "Monroe Doctrine." It contained two principal statements. The first statement, aimed at Russia, declared that the Western Hemisphere was no longer open to European colonization:

> The occasion has been judged proper for asserting as a principle in which the rights and interests of the United States are involved, that the American continents, by the free and independent conditions which they have assumed and maintain, are henceforth not to be considered as subjects for future colonization by any European powers (*Encyclopaedia Britannica,* p. 738).

The other chief point came near the end of his speech, when Monroe warned that the United States would consider as a hostile act any attempt by Europeans to "extend their system to any portion of this hemisphere" (Carson, p. 204).

For a new nation struggling to find its place among the world's powers, the Monroe Doctrine outlined a bold position with little military backing, except for the British navy. It amounted to a diplomatic declaration of independence. The United States had made its way to the stage of international politics and the Monroe Doctrine would remain the basis for American policy in the Western Hemisphere into the twentieth century.

Aftermath

South America, Mexico, and Alaska. The Monroe Doctrine had an immediate impact, possibly partly because European countries were soon entangled in internal defenses against republicanism. The restored monarchy in Spain did not take action to restore its position in Latin America. Many years later, as Spain lost its interest even in its holdings in Mexico, France intervened in that country. This occurred at a time when the United States had problems of its own, but as soon as these were resolved, the Monroe Doctrine was employed as the guide under which United States forces intervened, and diplomats succeeded in achieving the withdrawal of France from Mexico.

The idea of the Monroe Doctrine came into play again when the United States took charge of the Oregon Territory and California, overrunning Russian interests there. This eventually led to Russia's sale of Alaska to the United States, negotiated by United States Secretary of State **William Seward** (see entry).

Monroe. In 1824 Monroe left the United States presidency. Partisan politics had again become the password in American politics. Salaries for public officials were low in Monroe's day, and his years of public service left him with many debts. Eventually he was forced to sell his Virginia estate. Finally the government recognized his great work by voting him a payment of $30,000. It was too late. Monroe died a poor man in New York City, July 4, 1831.

For More Information

Ammon, Harry. *James Monroe*. Charlottesville: University Press of Virginia, 1990.

Carson, Clarence B. *The Beginning of the Republic*. Wadsey, Alabama: American Textbook Committee, 1984.

Cresson, W. P. *James Monroe*. Chapel Hill: University of North Carolina Press, 1946.

Encyclopaedia Britannica. 11th ed. [Chicago]. 1917.

Johnson, Allen. *Jefferson and His Colleagues*. New York: BCI One, 1992.

Perkins, Dexter. *Monroe Doctrine, 1826–1867*. New York: Peter Smith, undated.

Klemens Metternich

1773-1859

Personal Background

The Metternich-Winneburg family. Count Franz Georg Karl von Metternich-Winneburg zu Bellstein was a roving diplomat who worked wherever his services could be sold. His employers included the Catholic Archbishop of Trier and the Austrian ruler in Vienna. Eventually, he established a long service as Austrian ambassador to three small German states along the Rhine River.

In the count's travels he met Maria Beatrice Aloisia von Kagenezy, daughter of another noble family, and a marriage was arranged. Franz and Maria soon had a son who would one day have great influence on the French emperor Napoléon Bonaparte and even greater influence on the shaping of Europe after the French defeat. This son, Klemens Wenzel Nepomuk Lothar, who is known today simply as Klemens Metternich, was born May 15, 1773.

Early life and education. Life as a nobleman and diplomat's son came easy for Metternich. From an early age, he was made aware of his brilliance and became arrogant about his good looks and exceptional abilities. By the age of fifteen, he spoke and read several languages, including French and German, and was prepared to enter the University of Strassburg. (Strassburg, or Strasbourg, is now a French city near the Rhine River.) There he

▲ **Klemens Metternich**

Event: Inspiring the Monroe Doctrine.

Role: Austrian prime minister Klemens Metternich was the dominant leader in Europe after the defeat of French emperor Napoléon Bonaparte in 1814. His determination to restore the nations of Europe to their previous aristocratic forms included a plan to recapture former European colonies. His proposal to use force to regain Latin America for Spain led James Monroe to establish the Monroe Doctrine for the protection of all the Americas.

studied German law for two years before the civil unrest of the French Revolution reached the city. Amid the riots, Metternich abandoned the university and the city, but not before he had seen the wildly unruly behavior of the French revolutionaries first-hand. The horrors brought on by the undisciplined mob actions, unchecked by any strong government or law, were to remain a vivid influence on him throughout his life. From that time on, Metternich would be a champion of strong and autocratic governments.

The path to greatness. Metternich did so well during his two years at the university, and his manners and bearing were so aristocratic, that he was soon called to represent all the Catholic colleges of Westphalia (a province in Prussia) at the coronation at Frankfurt of Leopold II, emperor of Prussia. Two years later, in 1792, he served the same function at the coronation of Holy Roman Emperor Francis II. Between these two coronations, Metternich lived in the German city of Mainz and studied law there. It was a city to which many French were fleeing from the Revolution. The young diplomat listened to the terrible experiences of the refugees and became even more convinced that very strong governments were absolutely necessary to control and care for the masses of people.

The Real Metternich
Metternich grew to be a conceited, self-confident diplomat who, in the midst of his great career, described himself in his memoirs: "I am always above and beyond the preoccupation of most public men.... I cannot keep myself from saying about twenty times a day: 'How right I am, and how wrong they are.'" (Metternich in his memoirs, quoted in Bruenig, p. 170)

Marriage. By 1792, Metternich's father had become a foreign minister in Brussels, and Metternich joined him there as an assistant. Metternich served there just a short time before moving to England. Now intent on a political life, he returned from England to marry Countess Eleanore von Kunitz, granddaughter of the Austrian chancellor. The marriage made Metternich a wealthy landowner, and he became acquainted with other owners of great estates, who were also members of the elite society of Vienna. His aristocratic appearance made him popular among Vienna's leading families, and for the next few years he enjoyed the high society life while continuing to study—next taking up medicine and science.

Then in 1797 Metternich's diplomatic career began to flourish. He was elected Westphalian representative to the congress at Rastadt. Organized for the purpose of settling differences between France and the loosely organized German Empire, the congress achieved nothing, but Metternich emerged as a recognized leader. In short order, he followed this assignment with appointments as the Austrian representative in other European states.

Metternich and Napoléon. From the time he became ambassador in Paris in 1806, Metternich began a steady climb to become one of the European world's most important leaders. In Napoléon's court, his charm and self-confidence made him a favored person, though he served as a double agent. He was there to improve relations between France and Austria and to try to undermine Napoléon. In his second task, he would rely heavily on his own belief that the French people would soon weary of their dictator. Metternich was soon plotting with Napoléon's enemies at the same time as he was officially courting the dictator.

Rapid Rise of Metternich	
1801	Envoy to Saxony.
1803	Ambassador to Berlin.
1804	Ambassador to Russia.
1806	Ambassador to France upon the request of Napoléon.

Very shortly, Metternich began to realize that the French people would not rebel against their leader and feared that Napoléon could not be beaten. Metternich then began to focus on his duties as ambassador, though with very little success. By August 1806 Napoléon was angry with him and Austria because of Metternich's refusal to pledge Austria's direct support of the French president. Metternich was thrown into jail.

Released by Napoléon in exchange for some French diplomats held by Austria, Metternich returned to Vienna. He had now become a firm advocate of war to unseat Napoléon. He had also formed his own guiding principle for establishing a peaceful Europe—the principle he called "legitimacy." This policy would later cause **James Monroe** (see entry) to initiate the Monroe Doctrine, the U.S. policy of protecting existing governments in Latin America from further European interference.

▲ Napoléon Bonaparte; in Napoléon's court, Metternich's charm and self-confidence made him a favored person, though he served as a double agent.

Participation: Inspiring the Monroe Doctrine

Austrian foreign minister. Metternich returned to a broken Austria and became its foreign minister. (The French had occupied most of the lands of the Holy Roman Empire, leaving only the kingdom of Austria.) France had become such a powerful threat that Metternich temporarily abandoned his legitimacy policy to plead for peace with France. When Metternich was again unsuccessful, Francis II decided to negotiate with Napoléon directly. The results were painful to Austria. That great empire was restricted to an army of only 150,000 men, and Napoléon designated the parts of Austria from which these soldiers could come. In 1810 Metternich was able to reduce some of the French demands—mostly because France needed, at the least, Austrian neutrality in the coming war between Russia and France. Always placing the interests of Austria first, Metternich had agreed to supply France with a token army of thirty thousand for the war.

Russia and the Quadruple Alliance. By this time, several of the larger powers—Britain, Prussia, and Russia, among them—had decided to join in an alliance to resist the invasions of Napoléon's army. Metternich was afraid of a powerful Prussia, however, and refused to join the alliance. When Napoléon marched into Russia in 1812, the Russians fought a retreating battle while destroying all the materials that an invading army might use. When the French army arrived at Moscow, winter had already set in and Napoléon's troops were left without supplies. By the time they retreated to France, Napoléon's power had been shaken. Then Austria joined Britain, Prussia, and Russia in a Quadruple Alliance to finish the job of destroying Napoléon. When that task was nearly completed, the four great powers met for a series of conferences in Vienna from September 1814 to June 1815 to decide how to divide Europe.

> ## Whom Did Metternich Serve?
>
> The history of Metternich's governmental role is confused by the change of names of the ruler under which he served. Before the empire was dissolved by Napoléon, Emperor Francis II ruled over a large area of Europe known as the Holy Roman Empire. When that empire failed, Francis II held on to Austria and became Francis I, emperor of Austria.

Metternich's idea of "legitimacy" held that the old autocracies of Europe should be restored, and that these great powers had the right to intervene in smaller nations where royal rulers were threatened by rebellions. But first Austria must be protected, and Metternich engineered a postwar settlement that would create a long-standing balance among the big powers. Among his accomplishments were the creation of a Netherlands that included pre-

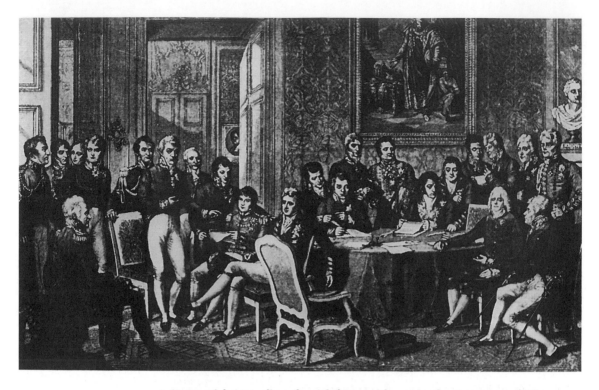

▲ Metternich (standing, front left) presides over the Congress of Vienna, 1815; after the downfall of Napoléon, the four great European powers met to decide how to divide Europe.

sent-day Belgium and Holland, and the restoring of France to its pre-Napoléon boundaries. France was again established as a monarchy.

Legitimacy in action. With a treaty that promised to preserve the Austrian Empire, Metternich could, for the next thirty years, practice his policy of legitimacy. In his view, it was appropriate, for example, for Austria to invade the kingdom of Naples and restore the old king who had been replaced by French leadership. It was also appropriate, in Metternich's mind, to authorize France, under its new king, to raise another army, invade the rebellious Spain, and restore that country to a monarchy.

It was also legitimate, Metternich felt, that the old monarchies of Europe should reclaim their earlier colonies. Metternich proposed that the European allies provide ships and troops to help Spain regain its colonies in Latin America.

Britain had just tried again to take back its American colonies in the War of 1812 and was not interested in new battles in America. It refused to help Metternich in his 1820 scheme, while at the same time sending an envoy to the United States to promote the idea that the new American republic would be endangered by Metternich's plans. The British proposed that the United States and Britain join hands in a declaration of opposition to Metternich's proposed move on Latin America. Certainly, Austria and its allies had the power to intervene in Latin America. A number of countries there were just gaining independence and were very weak from resistance to their Spanish leaders. The British offered to work with the United States to prepare a statement of their position against European reinvasion of the Americas.

Dates in South American History

1810	Argentina becomes independent.
1817	José de San Martin wins independence for Chile.
1819	Simón Bolívar wins independence for Columbia and leads revolutionary forces in Venezuela.

Monroe and the Metternich policy. President James Monroe listened to the British envoy. But the War of 1812 was still a powerful memory. The United States, Monroe felt, had no reason to trust Britain. The threat to South America might, however, expand northward and needed to be opposed. Monroe therefore decided to prepare a position statement without British help.

Aftermath

The Americas and Europe. Probably more because of Britain's support of the United States than because of Monroe's statement, European forces would remain out of the Americas until the late 1840s, when France would occupy Mexico while the United States prepared for civil war.

Under the arrangements set up by Metternich at the conference of Vienna, Europe's balanced powers would maintain their positions and boundaries for many years. Metternich continued to lead European decision-makers until well after the 1830s, although his power would slowly fade. In 1833, at the Treaty of Berlin, he was to engineer the last strong European verification of his program of legitimacy. Still, he had led Austria in its greatest hours, having become a sort of super-secretary of state in 1821 and state chancellor in 1824.

In 1835 the old emperor died and was replaced by his son, Ferdinand I. Austria was, at that time, ready for a less autocratic, more liberal form of government. Metternich, however, stuck to his idea of the divine right to rule of the old autocratic line and was able to convince Ferdinand to carry out the strict rule started by his father.

Unfortunately for Ferdinand, the government bureaucracy was rusty and in need of reform. Pressure for change grew, and in 1848 riots erupted in Vienna. Ferdinand was forced to relieve Metternich of his duties. Metternich fled to Britain but returned later to Vienna. The riots had only served to convince him that his defense of autocratic and stern government was the only way to rule the people. The growing demands for citizen participation in government failed to change his mind. Metternich died on June 11, 1859, no longer a government official, but still holding to his ideas of the divine right of monarchs and the principle of legitimacy.

> ## Monroe Doctrine Response to Metternich
>
> "We ... declare that we should consider any attempt on [the part of the Holy Alliance of Europe] to extend their system to any portion of this hemisphere as dangerous to [the United States's] peace and safety.... It is ... impossible, therefore, that we should behold such interposition in any form with indifference." (Monroe's December 2, 1823, address to Congress, *Encyclopaedia Britannica*, p. 738)

Personal grief. Metternich married three times, all three of his wives dying before him. They bore him several children, more than one-half of whom died during his lifetime.

The Monroe Doctrine. The brief declaration of the United States's interest in keeping America free of European influence (with the support of the British, who controlled the seas) kept European monarchs out of Latin America until another Napoléon sent troops to invade Mexico. Even then, as soon as it was free of other problems, the United States took action to oust the French from Mexico. The Monroe Doctrine remained the policy of American relations for a century.

For More Information

Bruenig, C. *The Age of Revolution and Reaction, 1789-1850.* 2nd ed. New York: Norton, 1970.

Encyclopaedia Britannica. 11th ed. [Chicago]. 1917.

Haas, Arthur G. *Metternich, Reorganization and Nationality, 1813-1818: A Story of Foresight and Frustration in the Rebuilding of the Austrian Empire.* New York: Coronet, 1963.

Sauvigny, G. de Berthier de. *Metternich and His Times.* London, England: Oxford University Press, 1962.

Schroeder, Paul W. *Metternich's Diplomacy at Its Zenith.* New York: Greenwood, 1962.

Seward, Desmond. *Metternich: The First European.* New York: Viking Penguin, 1991.

William Seward

1801–1872

Personal Background

Early life. William Henry Seward was born on May 16, 1801. His father, Samuel S. Seward, was a doctor and farmer in Florida, a town in southern New York. His mother was Mary Jennings Seward. The Sewards were prosperous enough to own slaves who worked the farm, and William, who was soon given the nickname "Harry," grew up in a comfortable household. Nevertheless, Florida was a small town whose only educational institution was a one-room school. There Seward studied as a young boy until he was transferred to a larger school in nearby Goshen. His progress through these schools seems to have been routine, for at the age of fifteen, he was prepared to enter college. He enrolled in Union College, a small liberal arts college in Schenectady, New York. There he achieved excellent grades, and after six years graduated with honors, gaining Phi Beta Kappa recognition for high academic performance.

The bar and politics. After graduating, Seward decided to study law. He completed his law studies within a year and was admitted to the New York bar. In a short time, he had joined a prominent law firm and fallen in love with the daughter of the owner. Frances Miller and William Seward were married in 1824. He was on his way to success as an attorney, but politics was rapidly becoming his chief interest. In the late 1820s he joined the

▲ **William Seward**

Event: Carrying out the Monroe Doctrine.

Role: As secretary of state under both Abraham Lincoln and Andrew Johnson, William Seward played a key role in upholding the Monroe Doctrine through skillful diplomacy. He not only prevented European intervention in the Civil War, he persuaded the French to leave Mexico and avoided Russian encroachment on the Pacific Coast through the purchase of Alaska.

Anti-Masonic Party, under which he ran for Congress but lost. (The Anti-Masons had arisen as a political party in New York after the disappearance of William Morgan, a former Mason who had written a book claiming to reveal the Mason's secrets. The Masons were thought to have murdered Morgan, and a movement arose in opposition to them). He did, however, prepare a series of resolutions that were adopted by the Anti-Masons at their national convention. By 1830 Seward, not yet thirty years old, had changed to the Whig Party and been elected to the New York state senate. Three years later, the impatient Seward would run for governor of New York, losing to a candidate of New York's largest political machine run by Martin Van Buren.

Success. Now temporarily out of political jobs, Seward decided to serve as agent for a real estate firm whose owners were trying to collect debts from their tenants. Seward's diplomacy usually led to a settlement satisfactory to both parties. He had become a well-known figure, and his popularity increased. He began once more to support the Whig Party. Seward's old friend Thurlow Weed, a newspaper publisher and a prominent party boss, supported Seward in a successful bid to be governor of New York.

Seward proved to be a good and progressive leader, helping to make prison and educational reforms and providing jury trials for fugitive slaves. He was reelected for a second two-year term but was soon heavily in debt. Political office, in those times, did not pay much. Seward decided not to run for a third term and returned to law practice to repair his finances. He would not be out of politics long. He was soon supporting Whig candidates, who in 1848 included presidential candidate Zachary Taylor. His strong role in Taylor's election earned him a seat in the United States Senate.

Antislavery supporter. As a senator, Seward made many speeches against slavery and was soon a leader of the antislavery senators. While working in the Senate, he changed parties to the new Republican Party, as did his old friend Weed. Seward's reputation as an antislavery spokesman, backed by Weed's political machine, made Seward a top candidate for president. The Republicans, however, chose to hold their nominating

▲ President Abraham Lincoln; Lincoln rewarded Seward for campaigning for him by making Seward his secretary of state.

convention in Illinois, the home state of Abraham Lincoln. Eventually, Lincoln won the nomination and the subsequent election. Seward and Weed both campaigned for Lincoln in the presidential race of 1860. Lincoln rewarded him by making Seward his secretary of state.

Civil War. The new president was immediately confronted with Southern secession. Seward gave the president several suggestions for managing the crisis before a war began. Lincoln took some of this advice, but not all. He did not, for example, withdraw federal troops from Fort Sumter, a fort that Seward thought could not be held.

Preventing foreign intervention in the war. When war finally broke out, Seward made it his main purpose to prevent European nations from entering the war or recognizing the Confederacy. Following the Monroe Doctrine, he claimed that the Civil War was a domestic problem and that foreign powers had no right to interfere. International law, however, allowed other nations to recognize regions with newly established governments. Seward claimed there was no recognizable government in the South. England, Spain, France, Holland, and Brazil then declared neutrality. But that amounted to support for the South since Southern ships could now enter foreign ports. There could, Seward argued, be no neutral nation since there was no declared war in progress.

Lincoln soon undermined that argument by ordering a blockade of Southern ports, a clear act of war.

The *San Jacinto* affair. The problem of keeping Europe out of the war was made more difficult when the United States warship *San Jacinto* stopped a British steamer in the Bahamas and seized two Confederate messengers on their way to plead for support from England and France. The British immediately sent eight thousand troops to Canada and demanded the release of the envoys. Earlier the

---

How to Handle a Rebellion

Seward wanted Lincoln to take action to prevent the coming Civil War. He suggested that the new president:

- Forget about offices to be filled and office-seekers for a time.

- Defuse European sentiments favoring the South by withdrawing naval ships from overseas.

- Evacuate Fort Sumter but reinforce Fort Pickins and other Gulf Coast forts.

- Take advantage of the moves of Spain and France to invade Haiti and the Dominican Republic by declaring war on the two European nations. Such a war, Seward argued, would unite the American people.

United States had made similar demands for their own messengers, but now many opposed the action. Eventually Seward convinced Lincoln to return the messengers and apologize to the British.

Throughout the war, Seward acted to ward off European intervention. When there was still doubt that the Union could win the war, he took the European ambassadors in Washington on a tour that showcased American industrial might. And later, when it was discovered that British shipyards were building two ships for the Confederacy, Seward protested so violently that the two ships were seized by the British government. Overall, the Seward strategy was a great success for the Union. Historian Norman Graebner gives this view of the importance of Seward's actions in the war:

Assassination

On April 5, 1865, Seward was severely injured in a carriage accident. Nine days later, President Lincoln was shot. About the same time, a would-be assassin allied with John Wilkes Booth entered Seward's home. He fought his way to the bed where Seward lay recovering from his accident and attacked him with a knife. Seward, however, survived, and his attacker was later caught and hanged.

> Europe's final refusal to involve itself in the American struggle was nothing less than a total vindication of Seward's diplomacy. Whatever the North's diplomatic advantages, he had understood them and exploited them with astonishing effectiveness (Graebner, p. 72).

Mexico. Upon returning to the State Department, now under President Andrew Johnson, Seward set out to deal with the French intervention in Mexico. It was a clear violation of the principles of the Monroe Doctrine, but the United States was still reeling from the Civil War and had little other recourse than to solve the problem with diplomacy.

During the war, the French, along with the Britons and Spaniards, had sent troops to Mexico to collect debts owed their citizens. Britons and Spaniards settled their differences and left, but the French stayed. They imported an Austrian prince, Maximilian, to rule over Mexico. Lincoln was deeply involved in the Civil War and did not want to provoke French intervention, so he did little to oppose the move. The very popular Civil War general Ulysses S. Grant argued that the solution was to send troops into Mexico, but Seward argued that he could get the French to leave without using force.

In 1866 Seward sent a general to France with specific instructions: "I want you to get your legs under Napoléon's mahogany and tell him he must get out of Mexico" (Temple, p. 108). By sending such a message through a military man, Seward was implying that continued French action in Mexico would result in, at least, unfriendly relations between France and the United States. French emperor Napoléon III (the nephew of Napoléon I) listened to the diplomats. He had enough problems warding off Prussia, which was expanding in Europe, and he agreed to withdraw French troops from Mexico. Maximilian's regime collapsed, and the Mexican republic was restored.

Alaska. Seward's greatest success during his years in the Johnson administration was the purchase of Russian America (although many at the time called it "Seward's Folly"). For half a century, the northwest corner of North America had been held by Russia and leased to the Russian American Company, a Russian trading company. The company's lease was due to expire in 1867. In spite of sometimes cruel exploitation of the native Alaskans, the territory had not proved profitable. Russia was faced with a dilemma. Should it renew the bad lease, organize an expensive colonial government, or sell the territory?

The Russian establishment of a colony in Alaska clearly violated U.S. interests as described in the Monroe Doctrine. Seward therefore directed Cassius M. Clay, his minister in St. Petersburg, to seek concessions in Russian America. Clay met with Russia's minister to the United States, Edouard de Stoeckl. Stoeckl had big plans—he wanted to sell the entire territory, which he saw as a liability for Russia. When he brought this idea to the Russian foreign minister, he approved.

Stoeckl returned to Washington and immediately began negotiations with Seward. Finally, a price was agreed upon. The United States would pay Russia $7.2 million for Alaska. In addition, the United States would pay the remaining debts of the Russian

American Company. The Russian government cabled its agreement to these terms, and Stoeckl immediately went to Seward's home to suggest that the two meet the next day to prepare a treaty. Seward, however, was so pleased that he could not wait, suggesting that they prepare the treaty that evening. Gathering the necessary assistants, along with Senator Charles Sumner, chairman of the Senate Foreign Relations Committee, an agreement was completed by 4:00 A.M. On April 9 the president submitted it to Congress. It was approved with only two negative votes. But getting the money to pay for the purchase was another matter. It took Seward and Stoeckl more than a year of hard lobbying, until, in July 1868, a bill for financing the purchase was finally approved by Congress. The United States purchased Alaska in 1868, and Seward had removed another foreign influence from the Americas.

Aftermath

Seward retired when Johnson left office. He began to travel widely, visiting Alaska, California, and Mexico, where he was an official guest of the republic he had helped preserve. He eventually traveled around the world. During his trip, his health began to fail. He seems to have suffered from a nervous disorder that affected the nerves to his muscles, gradually causing him to lose the use of both arms and making it impossible for him to eat without assistance. He did, however, begin to dictate his autobiography. On October 10, 1872, the disease finally caused his death.

For More Information

Graebner, Norman A. "Northern Diplomacy and European Neutrality." In *Why the North Won the Civil War,* edited by David Donald. New Orleans: Louisiana State University Press, 1960.

Latane, John Holladay. *A History of American Foreign Policy.* Revised and enlarged by David W. Wainhouse. Garden City, New York: Doubleday, Doran, 1934.

Taylor, John M. *William Henry Seward: Lincoln's Right Hand.* New York: Harper-Collins, 1991.

Temple, Henry W., and William H. Seward. *American Secretaries of State and Their Diplomacy.* Edited by Samuel Flagg Bemis. New York: Alfred Knopf, 1928.

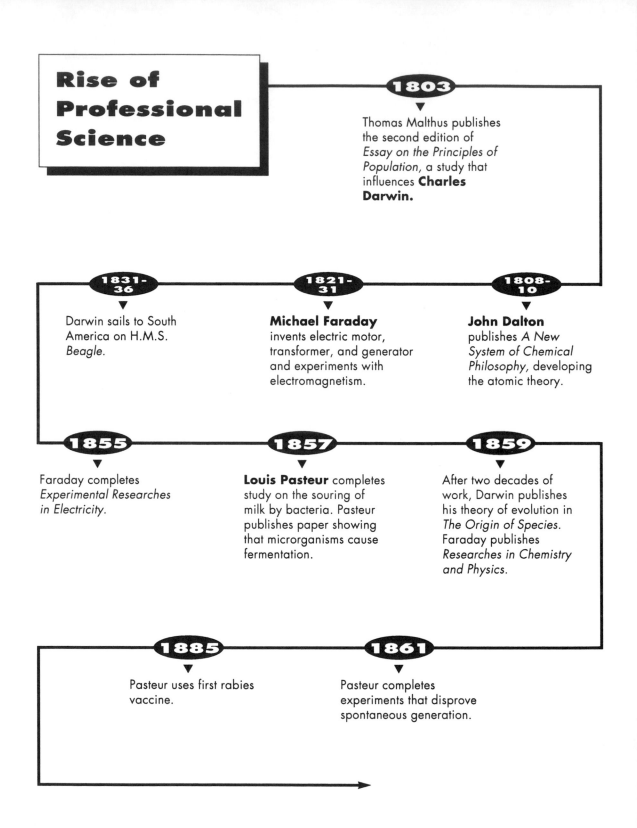

Rise of Professional Science

1803
▼
Thomas Malthus publishes the second edition of *Essay on the Principles of Population*, a study that influences **Charles Darwin.**

1831-36
▼
Darwin sails to South America on H.M.S. *Beagle.*

1821-31
▼
Michael Faraday invents electric motor, transformer, and generator and experiments with electromagnetism.

1808-10
▼
John Dalton publishes *A New System of Chemical Philosophy*, developing the atomic theory.

1855
▼
Faraday completes *Experimental Researches in Electricity.*

1857
▼
Louis Pasteur completes study on the souring of milk by bacteria. Pasteur publishes paper showing that microorganisms cause fermentation.

1859
▼
After two decades of work, Darwin publishes his theory of evolution in *The Origin of Species.* Faraday publishes *Researches in Chemistry and Physics.*

1885
▼
Pasteur uses first rabies vaccine.

1861
▼
Pasteur completes experiments that disprove spontaneous generation.

RISE OF PROFESSIONAL SCIENCE

During the eighteenth and nineteenth centuries, science in the West changed dramatically, both in the way it was practiced by scientists and in the way it was seen by society. Like many other changes in this two-hundred-year period, the changes in science can be seen as marking the arrival of a modern outlook.

The practice of science grew rapidly in the eighteenth century. Originally considered a branch of philosophy, it became first an established field in its own right, then a large area of study with its own smaller fields. Consequently, the people who practiced science stopped being philosophers and became scientists.

A respectable profession. By the nineteenth century, the way scientists themselves were viewed by society changed. For the first time, science had begun playing more than a supporting role on the stage of history. Society recognized science's growing importance in many ways, among them by giving scientists the ultimate in respectability: a place among the professions.

Respectability was very important for the growing middle class of the nineteenth century, and the height of respectability (for men) was to be a professional man—a lawyer or a doctor, for example. At the beginning of the nineteenth century science remained basically a hobby of upper-class gentlemen with intellectual interests and the free time to pursue them. It was practiced largely in the societies and clubs such gentlemen formed. The few scientists who could make a living in science were employed mostly in these societies, with only a handful in the universities. By the end of the century, however, science was a more widespread career option, one that brought not only a decent living (and sometimes wealth), but also public respect.

This new situation grew directly out of science's part in the Industrial Revolution, which changed life in the West starting in the late eighteenth century. These changes were all based on rapid improvements in technology; technology in turn was based on scientific knowledge and understanding. Yet it was a two-way street, for technology often spurred science to explore new problems. It was an age of invention, of progress, and of growing faith in the power of knowledge to improve the world. The scientist was one the new heroes of this age.

John Dalton's life took in the early part of these changes, showing the difficulties faced by scientists in these days. Dalton, who developed the modern theory of the atom, did his work on his own, while supporting himself by teaching. Even when he had won great public recognition for his important discoveries, he continued to work as a private teacher to the end of his life. He did not make his living from science, though in 1833 he was offered a house and a limited income from the government—long after he had done his most important work.

Michael Faraday met similar obstacles, overcoming them by getting one of the few jobs available in science. Beginning in 1813 Faraday worked for the Royal Institution in London, a leading scientific society. The gentlemen who were members of the society paid his wages. In the institution's laboratory, Faraday did his famous experiments with electricity and magnetism, showing that they were the same force, and invented the electric motor, the transformer, and the generator. Though his discoveries were not used during his lifetime, within a few decades of his death they were instrumental in beginning the electronic age that we live in today.

Although Dalton and Faraday won public acclaim for their work, as young men both faced problems in practicing science while trying to make a living. They were among the trailblazers who opened the way for later scientists.

Charles Darwin, by contrast, came from a wealthy family and had two famous grandfathers. Darwin did not have to worry about making his living from science or anything else. As a young man he had no firm idea of what he wanted to do and was pushed by his father toward "respectable" careers in medicine or religion. Only when he signed up for a sailing expedition to South America did his life come into focus.

From his observations of nature during the five-year voyage, Darwin made the most influential contribution ever to the field of biology: his theory of evolution. Not only did he revolutionize biology, but his theory's radical conclusions changed forever the way humankind viewed its place in the natural world. Darwin's ideas affected people's world outlook as deeply as Faraday's physics discoveries would later affect their daily lives. While the work of Dalton and Faraday won them fame, they themselves did not occupy the place in society of a Darwin, whose 1859 book *The Origin of Species* burst like a bombshell over the whole age. Challenged by religious authorities, Darwin's ideas remain highly controversial.

The work of French biologist **Louis Pasteur,** however, made him one of the age's undisputed public heroes. Like the universities, industry began giving money for research or funding positions at universities. Many of Pasteur's discoveries came from his connections with the important French wine and textiles industries. His ideas grew out of work on fermentation, the process by which wine is made. Aside from inventing a process (pasteurization) for preserving milk and other liquids, Pasteur developed vaccines for diseases such as rabies.

Pasteur's career shows how science had grown in importance since Dalton's time. No longer was science practiced only in gentlemen's societies.

John Dalton

1766-1844

Personal Background

Early life. John Dalton was born around September 6, 1766, in the small northern English village of Eaglesfield. His exact birthday is not known, because his birth was not registered in the village records. His parents, Joseph and Deborah Greenup Dalton, were Quakers, like many of Eaglesfield's families. Joseph was a weaver, and the family home was a small, two-room cottage. John and his brother and sister, Jonathan and Mary, went to a Quaker school, Pardshaw Hall School, about two miles from home.

An older Friend. Quakers call themselves the Society of Friends, and one of John's neighbors in Eaglesfield, the wealthy Elihu Robinson, proved a very good friend indeed to the young boy. Robinson was an enthusiastic scientist in his spare time, a man who exchanged letters with the likes of Benjamin Franklin and others who shared his interests. He was an amateur, but then this was an age before the rise of the professional scientist. In fact, the young boy whose intelligence Robinson noticed would do as much as anyone to bring about the rise of professional science. All that, however, was years in the future when Robinson first took John under his wing, explaining the latest scientific advances or giving him difficult math problems to solve.

Once, when a problem was especially tough, Robinson offered to show John the answer. John refused politely, saying

▲ **John Dalton**

Event: Origin of modern atomic theory.

Role: An English scientist and teacher, John Dalton began studying the weather as a young man. His early work in meteorology led him to wonder about the behavior of gases. From there he arrived at the idea that all elements, including gases, are made up of tiny particles that have the same weight and are in fact identical in each element. The atom was an old idea, going back to Greek times, but Dalton was the first to think of defining it by its "atomic weight"—an idea that is now the basis of modern chemistry.

that he preferred to solve it for himself. This same quiet stubbornness and independence would later lead him to some of his greatest breakthroughs. He never felt comfortable relying too much on the work of others.

Teacher. John wanted an education, but his family was so poor that they could not afford to keep him in school. By the time he was about ten, it was clear that he and Jonathan would soon have to do their share to help support the household. Taking a practical approach, John decided that if he couldn't attend school as a student, he would go as a teacher and learn that way. Luckily, the local school had just lost its teacher, and John was able to persuade them that he could do the job. At the age of twelve, therefore, he began teaching children only slightly younger than himself. After a year, however, he had made so little money teaching that he was forced to get work on local farms. Although two years of physical labor made his body strong, it offered little for his mind.

Meanwhile, John's older brother Jonathan had found a teaching job at a Quaker school in the town of Kendal, forty miles away in northern England's famous Lake District. Jonathan was able to arrange a job at the school for his younger brother. So in 1781, at the age of fifteen, John left for Kendal.

Kendal and John Gough. John taught elementary school in Kendal for twelve years. Within a few years, he and Jonathan were running the school, and their sister Mary had moved in to keep house for them. It was a time of growth and self-education for Dalton. Kendal was a larger and more exciting town than Eaglesfield and offered opportunities for him to explore and broaden his interests. There were public lectures by leading figures in science and mathematics. And there was John Gough, the famous blind scientist whose wisdom and knowledge were celebrated in William Wordsworth's poem *The Excursion*. Gough, also a Quaker, took a liking to Dalton. Like Robinson had earlier, Gough tutored the younger man carefully. He taught Dalton Latin, Greek, French, and mathematics, as well as the various branches of science, including chemistry and meteorology.

It was meteorology that first really sparked Dalton's interest. Following Gough's example, Dalton began keeping a daily record of the weather, in which he recorded barometric pressure, wind direction and velocity, rainfall, and other details. He wrote these things down faithfully every day for the rest of his life—by the time he died, his weather diary filled eleven volumes.

Participation: Origin of Modern Atomic Theory

Move to Manchester. By his early twenties, Dalton was not only going to public lectures in science but giving them as well. In 1790 he began to consider the next stage of his career. He decided that teaching offered little hope of fulfilling his ambitions to make a mark in the world, along with making some money. Yet becoming a doctor or lawyer, older friends like Robinson told him, was not a realistic goal for someone from such a poor family.

In 1792 Dalton was offered another teaching job, this time at a Quaker university recently established in Manchester, northern England's leading city. It was a big step up, and Dalton accepted eagerly. He moved to Manchester, and for the rest of the 1790s was very happy there, teaching mathematics and science, continuing to lecture in Kendal from time to time, and hiking in the Lake District's beautiful hills in the summer. He also took the important step of joining several scientific organizations, among them the Manchester Literary and Philosophical Society. The society would soon become one of the most prominent in England—just as Manchester itself would soon become England's second largest city, after London, during the coming industrial age.

Meteorological Observations. In 1793, just before joining the society, Dalton published his first major work, *Meteorological*

Science and the Industrial Revolution

Dalton's life spanned roughly the first half of the Industrial Revolution, in which a century (c.1780–c. 1880) of rapid breakthroughs in science and technology gave rise to the modern world's factories, assembly lines, and mass-produced goods. Such techniques were first developed in northern England, which became England's industrial heartland. Many advances can be traced to the wool trade and to weaving, traditionally the north's economic mainstay. Steam power, for example, was first used on a large scale to drive huge looms, machines on which wool was woven into cloth. Similarly, advances in chemistry came out of the need for better dyes and dyeing techniques. Dalton grew up just as such advances were gathering speed. In this atmosphere of excitement and discovery, scientists struggled to understand the principles on which the new technology was based.

Observations and Essays. He had written the book while still in Kendal, and it was mostly a summary of meteorological techniques—how to use instruments such as a barometer, for example, which measures the pressure of the atmosphere. Yet parts of the book show an original mind at work. For instance, in one section of the book he discusses the aurora borealis, the northern lights, concluding correctly that the strange glow of the aurora is caused by the earth's magnetic forces. And hidden in the parts of the book about the atmosphere were the seeds that would later grow into Dalton's theory of the atom.

Blue Eyes?

Though Dalton was the first to examine color blindness scientifically, his guess about the origins of the defect was wrong. He supposed the liquid inside his eyes to be blue, so that it absorbed red rays from light, preventing them from being seen. He left orders for his eyes to be dissected after his death, but when cut open they turned out to be normally transparent.

Color blindness. Dalton's subsequent work, however, had nothing to do with atoms, but remains important anyway. A few weeks after joining the society, Dalton read his first paper to its members. If he had never developed his atomic theory, this paper alone would have given him a place in science history, for Dalton had discovered color blindness. He himself was color blind, as was his brother. It was known, of course, that some people had difficulty telling certain colors apart. Yet no one had ever thought about the problem scientifically. Most Europeans call color blindness "Daltonism," but British scientists link Dalton's name to his other discoveries.

Dalton's law. Aside from his work on color blindness, Dalton spent the rest of the 1790s developing his ideas about meteorology. In 1800 he quit his teaching job, going into business for himself as a private teacher. In the meantime, he kept writing papers, most of which he read to the society or to similar groups in London. In them he discussed (among other things) the behavior of gases, an issue he had also raised in his *Observations*. There he suggested that air is simply a mixture of gases, not a chemical compound of them, as was commonly believed. In other words, he claimed, air is made up of separate gases that keep their own identities even though mixed up together. But he had only mentioned this idea briefly.

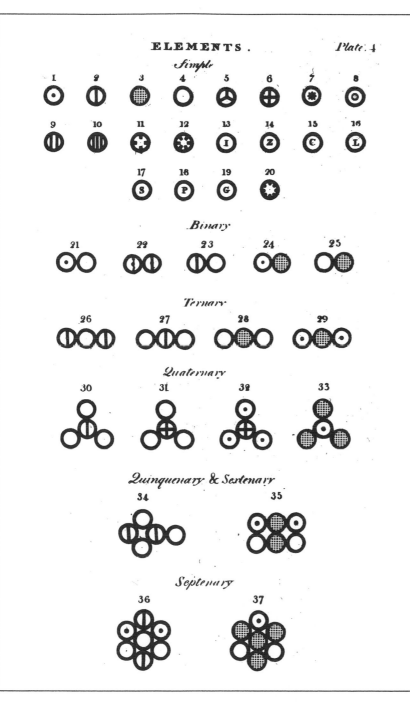

▲ Dalton's depiction of the chemical elements from his *New System of Chemical Philosophy;* Dalton showed in his experiments that atoms always combine in simple ratios: 1 to 1, or 2 to 1, or 2 to 3, for example.

In 1801, however, Dalton published several articles developing the idea further and backing it up with experiments. This time, the scientific world paid more attention. The theory he now put forward later became known as Dalton's law, or the Law of Partial Pressures. It says that the total pressure of a mixture of gases equals the sum of the pressures of each individual gas in the mixture. In other words, each gas in the mixture can be thought of as acting independently, with a pressure the same as if the other gases were absent. All the separate pressures can be added up to get the total pressure of the mixture as a whole.

From gases to atoms. While some supported Dalton's idea, many—including his old friend John Gough—attacked it. They still preferred to think of gases as a single substance rather than as a mixture. In defending the theory, Dalton was forced to look more closely at some of the details in his own work. In particular, in order to prove that gases were not a chemical compound or combination, Dalton had to consider what such a compound itself was. He had to define what he was *not* talking about, in order to show what he *was* talking about. He had to enter the world of chemistry.

In 1801 and 1802 Dalton mentioned one idea in several lectures almost casually. It was an old idea, but he added a new twist that in the end changed science forever. The idea of the atom, the "uncuttable" (*atomos*) smallest possible bit of matter, had come from the ancient Greek philosophers. It had been discussed by many scientists of Dalton's day and earlier. Dalton's new twist was to describe how atoms behaved, basing his description on modern science's central idea, measurement—in this case, measurement of weight.

New System. Bit by bit, experiment by experiment, Dalton developed the new theory. Slowly, too, he became more and more aware of its revolutionary possibilities. What had begun as a defense of one idea had grown into a much bigger idea in its own right. By 1808, when he published Part I of his book *A New System of Chemical Philosophy,* the basic ideas were in place; with Part II, published two years later, he worked out some of the remaining details. Further advances would have to wait until decades after Dalton's death.

Dalton's theory was that each element's atoms were identical to each other in size and weight. Since hydrogen is the lightest known element, he assigned it an "atomic weight" of 1. "Compound atoms" (later called molecules) were formed when the atoms of one or more elements combined. Dalton also showed in his experiments that the atoms always combined in simple ratios: 1 to 1, or 2 to 1, or 2 to 3, for example. That is, molecules are made up of predictable proportions that will always be the same. Ironically, the most famous proportion of all, that of water, he got wrong. He gave it as one atom of hydrogen and one of oxygen, when, of course, it has two atoms of hydrogen and one of oxygen: H_2O.

Aftermath

Growing fame. Though the atomic theory could not be proved until the development of better scientific instruments, it soon began to win supporters in the scientific community. Some, including Dalton himself, suggested systems of symbols for the various elements. The simple system of letters and numbers (for example, H_2O) later adopted was not his version. Dalton worked hard for another twenty-five years, filling out the table of known atomic weights by carrying out further experiments. In its final version, this table has become the basic tool of modern chemistry, the science of how substances interact with each other. As his theory gained acceptance, this quiet and modest man became England's most famous scientist of the day. Despite his fame, he continued his teaching. Dalton died on July 27, 1844, at his home in Manchester.

For More Information

Greenaway, Frank. *John Dalton and the Atom.* London: Heinemann, 1966.

Thackray, Arnold. *John Dalton: Critical Assessments of His Life and Science.* Cambridge, Massachusetts: Harvard University Press, 1972.

Michael Faraday

1791-1867

Personal Background

Early life. Michael Faraday was born in London, England, on September 27, 1791. His father, James Faraday, was a blacksmith whose health problems often prevented him from working. His mother, Margaret Hastwell Faraday, was a farmer's daughter from northern England, where the two had met and married before moving to London.

Sandemanians. James Faraday's family belonged to a small Protestant religious sect called the Sandemanians, after its founder, Robert Sandeman. The Sandemanians held beliefs somewhat similar to those of the Quakers, seeking to live by Christian principles as expressed in the Bible. They stressed church attendance and simple living. Faraday raised his children, of whom Michael was the third, according to these ideas. Throughout his life, Michael held deep religious beliefs and kept up Sandemanian practices—even though later in his life he was briefly expelled from the sect for going to dinner with the Queen one Sunday instead of to church. He didn't mind, for there were only two things stronger than his religious faith: one was his independence, the other was his curiosity.

Bookbinder's apprentice. Dinner with the Queen would have seemed like an impossible dream amid the poverty of Faraday's boyhood. James's poor health kept the family short of

▲ Michael Faraday

Event: Discovery of electromagnetism.

Role: Michael Faraday is often called the greatest experimental scientist of all time. In a series of brilliant experiments, he confirmed that the forces of electricity and magnetism are in fact a single force and showed how it works. He also invented the electric motor, the transformer, and the generator, three devices that became the basis of the electrical age after his death.

money, and at the age of thirteen Michael was forced to leave school and go to work. For a year, he delivered newspapers for a bookseller named George Riebau. At the end of this trial period, Riebau took Michael on as an apprentice. Moving into a room over the bookshop, Michael learned how to bind the books between stiff leather covers. And as he bound the books, he read them. He began keeping careful notes in his neat, precise handwriting. When he had enough notes, he bound them as a book, too, so he could study them easily. With Riebau's encouragement, he also read as many other books as he could get his hands on.

Royal Institution. After reading an article about electricity in the *Encyclopaedia Britannica,* Michael became fascinated with this mysterious form of energy. He began to read more and more about it. By his late teens, he had set up a simple lab in his room and was carrying out experiments to see if his own results would agree with what he read. He also began going to lectures on science, where he made friends his own age with similar interests. And always he kept careful notes. When he showed them to Riebau one day, the older man was impressed. Riebau in turn showed the notes to one of his best customers, a gentleman named Mr. Dance. Dance was a bit of an amateur scientist, like many gentlemen with time to spare, and asked to meet Michael. He told Michael that the famous scientist Sir Humphry Davy would be giving a series of lectures soon at the Royal Institution of London, a leading scientific organization to which Dance belonged. Dance then changed the course of history by offering Michael tickets to the lectures.

Sir Humphry. Faraday sat riveted through Davy's four lectures. As always, he took careful notes, and when the lectures were over, he copied them all over again, making careful drawings of the scientific instruments with which Davy carried out his demonstrations. Then he bound the notes and illustrations into a book, studying it over and over to make sure he understood everything.

His apprenticeship was coming to an end, and Michael now faced some tough choices about his future. On the one hand, he knew he could make a living as a bookbinder. On the other hand,

▲ **Sir Humphry Davy; as Davy's assistant, Faraday made his share of discoveries in the fast-growing field of chemistry.**

his scientific curiosity demanded satisfaction. He wanted to be a scientist, or rather a philosopher, as it was still called in those days. Science was just beginning to become a profession. And that was the problem: science wasn't yet generally seen as a way of making a living. It was still largely a pastime for gentlemen with money and leisure. Only a few bright stars without money could attract the support of such gentlemen, who would pay to pursue their hobby. In fact, Davy himself was such a star, a man from a background of poverty who had risen to his current status by his intelligence. He had not been born "Sir" Humphry, but had been given the title for his work in science—work supported by the upper-class gentlemen who were members of groups like the Royal Institution.

Occupational Hazards

When Faraday sent Davy his letter and notes, the famous scientist was recovering from a lab explosion which had temporarily damaged his eyes. Such explosions soon became a routine part of Faraday's workday. As Faraday wrote to a friend a few months after taking the job at the Royal Institution:

> I have escaped (not quite unhurt) from four different and strong explosions…. Of these the most terrible was when I was holding between my thumb and finger a small tube containing $7\frac{1}{2}$ grains of it [nitrogen trichloride]…. The explosion was so rapid as to blow my hand open, tear off a part of one nail, and has made my fingers so sore that I cannot yet use them easily (Kendall, p. 35).

"Bold and simple step." Faraday didn't hesitate. Knowing that Davy had left London (on his honeymoon) after the lectures, Faraday wrote a letter to Sir Joseph Banks, the president of another scientific group, the Royal Society of London. He never got an answer—indeed, when he called on Banks, a butler told him simply "No reply," meaning that Banks had no reply to make to the letter.

Undiscouraged, Faraday waited until Davy was back in town. Then, as he wrote later, "[I took] the bold and simple step of writing to Sir H. Davy expressing my wishes ... at the same time, I sent the notes I had taken of his lectures" (Kendall, p. 32). Davy met with Faraday, but informed him that, unfortunately, there was no job available at the Royal Institution. He already had an assistant, but he would be happy to send any books he needed bound to Michael. Shortly afterward, the assistant got into a fight with another employee and was fired. Davy immediately offered Faraday the job.

Participation: Discovery of Electromagnetism

Early years. When Faraday began working at the Royal Institution in 1813, he was twenty-one. He would remain there for the rest of his career, becoming the director of its laboratory in 1825. For the first several years, he helped Davy with various chemistry experiments. He lived in two rooms on the top floor of the Institution. In 1814 and 1815 he accompanied Davy and his wife on a long trip to Europe. The journey, though fascinating because Faraday met many European scientists, also became a bit of a nightmare for him. Davy's snobbish wife insisted on treating him like a personal servant. In general, though, Faraday was very happy working for Davy. It was a busy life with long hours and lots of excitement—sometimes, when working with dangerous chemicals, a little more excitement than even Faraday might have bargained for.

Oersted's discovery. As Davy's assistant, Faraday made his share of discoveries in the fast-growing field of chemistry. Then, in 1820, came news from Denmark that shifted his attention back to his former interest in electricity. A Danish scientist, Hans Christian Oersted, announced his discovery that an electric current, if passed through a wire placed near a compass needle, could make the needle move. In other words, electricity somehow creates a magnetic force, since a compass needle is moved by magnetism. It was the first time that a direct connection between the two forces had been confirmed experimentally.

Marriage. At around the time he began his struggle to understand electro-magnetism, Faraday met Sarah Barnard, also a Sandemanian, and the younger sister of a friend of his. A few years earlier, Faraday had written a joking poem against love, calling it "the pest and plague of human life." No sooner had he met Barnard than her mischievous brother gave her a copy of the poem. It took Faraday a long time to explain it away, but he succeeded, and the two were married in June 1821. It was a perfect match, and though they never had any children, two of Barnard's nieces lived with them for years. The marriage was long and happy.

First electric motor. Meanwhile, Davy and Faraday had been hard at work on their own experiments with wires and compasses, trying to get the same results as Oersted—and, at the same time, trying to figure out what those results meant. In the

---

Poles and Charges

A common bar magnet has two ends, one called the north pole and the other called the south pole. Similarly, electricity has a positive charge and a negative charge. The north poles of two magnets will repel each other, like their south poles, while the north pole of one magnet and the south pole of another will attract each other. In 1785 the French scientist Charles de Coulomb discovered that the same situation is true for positive and negative electrical charges. Like poles and charges attract each other; opposite poles and charges repel each other.

summer of 1821 Faraday was asked to write a summary of everything that was known about the new field of electromagnetism. Clearly, the forces somehow acted over a distance, sending out some kind of invisible push or pull on each other. Since ancient times, it was known that magnets mysteriously attracted certain metals. Similarly, the resinous substance called amber (*elektron* in Greek), when rubbed with fur, was known to attract things like feathers. But how did these seemingly almost magical forces actually work?

Faraday's first major breakthrough came in an experiment he made in early September. He filled a bowl with mercury and put a magnet upright in the middle, with the top just above the surface. Over it he hung a wire whose lower end, tipped with cork, floated in the mercury just beside the top end of the magnet. The upper end was connected to the positive terminal of a battery. Taking another piece of wire, he attached one end to the battery's negative terminal and put the other over the side of the bowl into the mercury. When it touched the mercury, the electrical circuit was completed, and the corked end of the wire began moving in a circle around the magnet. Faraday had converted electrical energy into mechanical movement. In other words, he had invented the electric motor.

Dynamo. Faraday kept up his experiments, and slowly, over the next decade, his understanding of electromagnetism grew. Soon after his invention of the electric motor, he invented the transformer, which is still used to change the voltage of an electrical current. Then, after improving his electric motor, he began experiments on reversing the process that made it work. If an electric current plus a magnet could produce mechanical movement, he reasoned, then mechanical movement plus a mag-

Lines of Force and Electromagnetic Fields

Faraday's principle of induction relied on his ideas about how electromagnetism acts on objects across empty space. He believed that what he called "lines of force" make up a "field," such as the field around a magnet. Induction relies on "breaking" these lines of force, converting the energy of a magnetic field into electrical energy in the material (a copper disk or wire) that is passed through the field.

An easy way to see Faraday's lines of force is to put a magnet under a flat piece of paper, sprinkle iron filings on top, and tap the paper gently. The filings will scatter along the lines, showing the magnet's field. Faraday's idea of an electromagnetic field was put into mathematical form after his death by the Scottish physicist James Clerk Maxwell, giving rise to field theory, a cornerstone of today's physics.

net should be able to produce a current. During a decade of work, Faraday came up with a scientific principle called induction, which explained how such a current might be produced. In 1831, ten years after the first two inventions, came a third: the dynamo, or generator, which produced electricity by moving a magnet through a coil of wire. Faraday's dynamo proved that induction worked. It is still the most important way of creating electricity.

Aftermath

Declining health. The decade beginning in 1821 was Faraday's most creative period, though he continued after that to come up with new ideas and experiments to test them. In the 1830s, for example, he developed techniques for electroplating, or depositing a thin layer of one metal over another by means of electricity. This technique is still used to make tin cans, or to coat a cheap metal with an expensive one like gold or silver. By the 1840s, however, Faraday's health began to suffer from the years of hard work, and in 1845 he had what seems to have been a nervous breakdown of some sort. By the 1850s he had to stop his experiments, and in 1861 he stopped teaching. Still, from 1839 to 1855 he wrote and published a three-volume work titled *Experimental Researches in Electricity* explaining his work and ideas. Faraday died on August 27, 1867, at the age of seventy-five.

For More Information

Brophy, Michael. *Michael Faraday.* New York: Bookwright Press, 1991.

Gutnick, Martin J. *Michael Faraday: Creative Scientist.* Chicago: Children's Press, 1986.

Kendall, James. *Michael Faraday: Man of Simplicity.* London: Faber and Faber, 1955.

Charles Darwin

1809–1882

Personal Background

Privileged upbringing. Charles Robert Darwin was born on February 12, 1809, in the southern English town of Shrewsbury. He came from a distinguished family, for both his grandfathers were wealthy and successful men. They were also good friends. Erasmus Darwin, philosopher, naturalist, inventor, and writer of widely read love poems, shared his liberal, "free-thinking" outlook with Josiah Wedgwood, founder of the famous pottery company. Their close friendship made it only natural for two of their children, Robert Darwin and Susannah Wedgwood, to marry each other. Charles was the fourth child of this union. Aside from his older brother Erasmus ("Eras"), Charles had four sisters, three older and one younger. Caroline, one of the older sisters, cared for him after their mother's death when Charles was eight.

"Shooting, dogs, rat-catching." The Charles Darwin later known to the world, with his long white beard and serious expression, was a far cry from the boyhood version. Actually, even the serious expression he wore for photographs was deceiving, for Darwin always kept the playful nature of his youth. Like Albert Einstein, a later scientist who also revolutionized people's view of the world, Darwin as a boy held out little promise of his future achievements. No one expected much of him, for he didn't do well in school and had little ambition.

▲ **Charles Darwin**

Event: Theory of natural selection.

Role: English naturalist Charles Darwin was not the first scientist to argue that life "evolved," or changed form over generations. He was, however, the first to offer a detailed scientific idea suggesting how evolution might take place. The idea, which he called "natural selection," appeared in his 1859 book, *On the Origin of Species and the Descent of Man,* considered one of the most influential scientific writings of all time.

▲ An 1840 watercolor of Darwin by George Richmond; the serious expression he wore for portraits was deceiving, for Darwin always kept the playful nature of his youth.

Only a few things stirred Darwin to passion. The outdoors was one. He loved hunting birds, hiking, and riding. Another was collecting—postage franks (like stamps), small animals, odds and ends useless to anyone but himself, and especially bugs. His father, Darwin later wrote, once told him, "You care for nothing but shooting, dogs, and rat-catching, and you will be a disgrace to yourself and all your family" (Darwin 1993, p. 28).

Beetling. When Charles was sixteen, his father sent him to Edinburgh, Scotland, to study medicine, but Charles was disgusted after watching an operation. Bored with classes, he spent his time combing the seashore for shells and other examples of ocean life. Ignoring medicine, he learned to stuff animals from a black ex-slave he met named John Edmonstone. Edmonstone, a well-traveled man, thrilled the teenager with tales of the South American rainforest. When Charles could no longer stick it out in Edinburgh, his father sent him to join Eras at Cambridge University. Now intended by his father to study to become a minister, he found little enthusiasm for the religious life. His main pursuit was "beetling"—collecting all the beetles he could find in competition with friends.

Henslow. Though generally bored in the classroom, in both Edinburgh and Cambridge Charles developed friendships with teachers who shared his enthusiasm for nature. In Edinburgh it had been Robert Grant, who studied sponges and followed the ideas of radical scientists such as the French biologist Jean-Baptiste Lamarck. Like Charles's grandfather Erasmus, Lamarck supported evolution, the idea that animals and plants had changed over the generations into new forms.

At Cambridge Darwin became friends with John Stevens Henslow, who taught botany, the study of plants. Darwin attended Henslow's lectures, and Henslow took him for long nature walks, on which they collected new or interesting species of flowers and shrubs. Henslow gave him books like Alexander von Humboldt's true story of South American exploration, *Personal Narrative*. Henslow was also a minister, the kind Darwin was beginning to think he himself might become—a man who observed religion but worshipped nature.

Fitzroy and H.M.S. *Beagle*. Soon after graduating in 1831, Darwin heard that Henslow had recommended him for a position on a sailing ship going to South America. The ship's captain, Robert Fitzroy, was looking for a gentleman to keep him company on the long voyage. The customs of the day prevented captains from mixing socially with the crew, who were of a lower social class. Fitzroy also wished to make the voyage a scientific one, so he wanted a man with a background in science, though there was already an official ship's naturalist. Henslow wrote to Darwin, "You are the very man they are in search of" (Desmond and Moore, p. 101).

Darwin's father opposed the idea as a waste of time, but he gave in when one of Charles's Wedgwood uncles argued in favor of it. So on December 27, 1831, after many delays and one false start because of bad weather, Darwin set sail on the H.M.S. *Beagle*. He was almost twenty-two years old. He had no idea when—or even if—he would be back.

Participation: Theory of Natural Selection

Destination: South America. The *Beagle* was a naval warship, carrying ten cannons, and the voyage was officially a military one. Its mission—two years minimum, with no set date of return—was to survey the coastal waters of South America. By the second day, Darwin was seasick. He was disgusted, too, by the whippings Fitzroy was already handing out as punishment to crew members. Soon, however, as he got used to shipboard life, Darwin began to enjoy his adventure. The journey turned out to last five years.

Dangerous science. Darwin's love of outdoor life served him well, for he got used to jumping on horseback and going off on long collecting trips when the ship anchored. Several times he left the *Beagle* and arranged to meet it farther on, traveling overland hundreds of miles in between. His trips were often dangerous, or at least adventurous. He climbed mountains, crossed swollen rivers, slept in the open, got bitten by giant bugs, and ate roasted armadillo for supper. He witnessed volcanic eruptions, survived a major earthquake, dug up huge fossils of long-vanished animals, and noted the remains of seashells in the mountains thousands of feet above sea level. When space on board ran out, he sent crates and crates of samples back to England. He met "savages" in the southern wilds of Tierra del Fuego and elsewhere along the coast—the native Indians with whom Spanish-descended settlers and soldiers were constantly battling, when they weren't battling each other. And all the time, he observed, made notes, and collected samples of the strange, wonderful, and often violent world through which he was journeying.

Lyell and deep time. Among the many books that Henslow had given Darwin to read on the trip was *Principles of Geology* by Charles Lyell. Lyell had published the book in 1830, shortly before Darwin left England. Like Lamarck, Lyell went against established ideas in the scientific world, many of which were based on religion and on parts of the Bible that seemed to deal with issues like the age and origin of the earth. From these Biblical stories, scientists had decided that the world must be very young—not much more than a few thousand years old. They accounted for evidence of change (for example, in rock formations) by concluding that there had been an early period of rapid, violent transformation.

Lyell claimed instead that much slower processes were responsible, changes like erosion and the gradual uplifting of the ground after small earthquakes. These processes, Lyell argued, were the same ones that could still be observed slowly changing the earth. If Lyell was right, the earth must be much, much older than was commonly believed, almost unimaginably old. (Lyell was right, as it turned out, and his ideas formed the basis of modern geology.)

As he compared Lyell's ideas with his own observations, Darwin, too, began to think in terms of small, slow changes taking place over vast immeasurable stretches of time.

Return and reflection. After sailing around South America's tip, up the coast of Chile, and across the Pacific to Australia, the *Beagle* continued on around the world, landing in England in October 1836. Happy to be back among the comforts of home, Darwin began the massive task of digesting all that he had seen on the five-year voyage. He had so many questions, so many ideas.

Environment, distribution, extinction. Despite a few supporters of evolution, such as Lamarck, most scientists believed

firmly that species did not change over time. They had been created, most believed, by God, and remained as God's unchanged creations. Darwin himself had at first accepted this view. Yet, according to Lyell, the earth itself had changed over time. Why would God create unchanging creatures to live on a changing world? Why did species that were clearly somehow related live in areas that were close together? And what about the huge fossils Darwin had found, fossils of animals no longer living? The huge animals themselves no longer survived, but Darwin noticed striking similarities in bone structure between the extinct animals and some smaller animals still living. It was almost as if the living animals were smaller, later versions of the larger ones. What did these similarities mean? Darwin asked himself such questions as he organized his samples and notes. It was not long before an answer came.

Lamarck's "Acquired Characteristics"

Lamarck had argued that animals evolved through their behavior. Thus, giraffes had long necks because earlier giraffes had developed them by reaching for food that was high off the ground. Similarly, Lamarck believed, a weightlifter's large muscles would be passed on to his children. These "acquired characteristics"— abilities formed by behavior—shaped evolution, according to Lamarck. Darwin rightly rejected this idea. Acquired characteristics are clearly not passed on to future generations.

Evolution—but how? Within a year or so after the *Beagle*'s return, Darwin accepted evolution over time as the answer to these and many other similar questions. After all, the idea had been around long enough. While still not generally accepted, it was no longer quite as radical as it had been in his grandfather's day. Yet accepting evolution was not a real answer, for the question immediately arose: how did it work?

Natural selection. Darwin based his answer on three simple observations. First, he recognized that all living organisms produce more offspring than can possibly survive. Second, among the offspring there are always some variations, small differences from the parents. Third, these small differences are

◀
One of the Galapagos Islands, on the Equator about six hundred miles west of Ecuador; all during his travels, Darwin observed, made notes, and collected samples of the strange, wonderful, and often violent world through which he was journeying.

passed on to future generations, along with inherited similarities. These observations were not new. What was new was the way Darwin combined them.

Darwin argued that the chance differences among the offspring actually play a role in determining which offspring survive. One baby giraffe might have a slightly longer neck, just by chance, than other giraffes. This difference would allow it to compete more successfully for food, giving it a better chance of survival—and of passing its longer neck along to its own offspring. Nature can be seen as "selecting" long-necked giraffes for survival. This principle of "natural selection," Darwin suggested, was what guided evolution. Natural selection is also called "survival of the fittest," meaning that the individuals whose chance differences best fit the environment (like longer-necked giraffes on plains with high trees) have the best chance of survival. Thus, two factors lie behind inherited change: chance and local environment.

Alfred Russell Wallace. Though he had hit upon his idea by the late 1830s, Darwin knew that society would have trouble accepting it. Above all, the idea of chance playing such an important role would go against most people's ideas that God, not chance, had created all forms of life and that humans were put in a special position of superiority. Natural selection suggested that humans were like other animals—a product of chance differences, not divine creation.

Darwin worked on his ideas in private for almost two decades, sharing them only with a few other scientists. Before he made his theory of natural selection public, he wanted to be able to support it with so much evidence that it would be hard to reject. In the meantime, he married his cousin Emma Wedgwood in 1839 and raised a family. He also pursued other work, writing several groundbreaking books about barnacles, for example.

In 1858 Darwin received a letter from a young naturalist named Alfred Russell Wallace. Darwin was shocked as he read a short version of his own idea! Wallace had come up with natural selection independently. At the suggestion of Darwin's friends, Darwin and Wallace joined forces and presented the idea together to an important scientific organization in London in July 1858.

Darwin now struggled to finish his own version, which was much more detailed than Wallace's. In November 1859 he published it in book form as *The Origin of Species by Means of Natural Selection.*

Aftermath

Controversies. Darwin had been right about public reaction to his idea. Yet he had prepared his material carefully, and the book sold out right away. In the end, its monumental achievement was to establish evolution as a scientific theory and to suggest natural selection as a possible instrument of change. The theory of evolution has inspired many investigations in science, as well as religious and social controversies. Both scientists and non-scientists have challenged Darwin's ideas from the moment he introduced them.

Darwin himself tried to stay out of the many public debates that followed, leaving the debates up to his supporters. The best known of them was Thomas Henry Huxley, often called "Darwin's Bulldog" for his public role in supporting natural selection.

Darwin, however, continued to publish books building on his revolutionary idea, and slowly it won acceptance in the scientific world. Religious objections, by contrast, were continuously mounted against it. Yet when he died on April 19, 1882, at seventy-three, Darwin was acclaimed as one of the greatest scientists of all time. He was honored by burial in London's Westminster Abbey, the burial place of another ground-breaking scientist, Isaac Newton.

For More Information

Darwin, Charles. *The Autobiography of Charles Darwin.* Edited by Nora Barlow. Reprint. New York: Norton, 1993.

Darwin, Charles. *The Origin of Species,* 1859. Reprint, edited by J. H. Borrow. New York: Penguin Books, 1982.

Darwin, Charles. *The Voyage of the Beagle.* New York: Harper and Row, 1959.

Desmond, Adrian, and James Moore. *Darwin. The Life of a Tormented Evolutionist.* New York: Norton, 1991.

Louis Pasteur

1822–1895

Personal Background

Early life. Louis Pasteur was born on December 27, 1822, in the eastern French town of Dole, not far from the city of Dijon. His father was a tanner, a craftsman who prepared leather for use in clothes, shoes, and equipment. Louis was the only boy, but he had several sisters with whom he was very close.

Art or science? When he was a young boy, his family moved to nearby Arbois, a larger town than Dole. There Louis grew up and attended elementary school. He was a good student, but not exceptional. Still, during his school days he always had the idea that he would end up as a professor. His family encouraged him, because becoming a professor would be a fine achievement for a tanner's son from a small country town. Professors were highly respected in French society.

Louis's strongest passion as a boy was painting and drawing. He practiced hard and had a lot of talent, producing detailed and accurate portraits of his family and friends. When he was sixteen he decided briefly that he would be a painter, maybe a professor of art. But another interest caught up with him during his college years. At nineteen he earned his bachelor of science degree and put down his drawing pen and paint brush forever. He decided to be a scientist.

Crystals and light. The following year, he applied for graduate studies in science at the École Normale Supérieure, the

▲ **Louis Pasteur**

Event: Development of germ theory.

Role: French scientist Louis Pasteur discovered that microscopic organisms (yeast) cause fermentation, the process by which beer and wine are made. His breakthroughs in fermentation led him to develop a technique (pasteurization) for killing bacteria, another kind of microorganism, in milk or similar liquids. He then discovered that bacteria, along with other germs called viruses, cause infectious diseases. Pasteur's discoveries about germs—bacteria and viruses—enabled him, in the final years of his life, to develop the first vaccines for many diseases.

famous school for teachers in Paris. Coming in sixteenth in the entrance exams, he was accepted, but sixteenth wasn't a good enough result for the demanding Pasteur. He went back and studied on his own for a year. Next year he placed fifth, after which he allowed himself to enter graduate school.

After several years of studies and research, he won his doctor of philosophy degree in 1847. His teachers and friends at the École had been working on a new area of study: the makeup of crystals and how they affect light that passes through them. For his degree, Pasteur also studied crystals and light. The crystals he studied were those found suspended in two kinds of acid: tartaric acid, commonly formed while making wine, and racemic acid, a new acid that had been found to result rarely in winemaking.

Discovery. Pasteur's work on these acids led to his first discovery, a major one that started his scientific career with a bang. Both acids had the same chemical composition and structure. They were different only in how they affected polarized light. (Normally light waves vibrate in many directions. Polarized light waves vibrate in one direction only.) Tartaric acid changed the direction of polarized light that was passed through its crystals, while racemic acid did not. How could this be, Pasteur wondered, if they were chemically identical? With a series of careful experiments, Pasteur showed that racemic acid actually had two kinds of crystals. One was exactly identical to those in tartaric acid. The other, however, was the mirror-image of the first. The two contained the same atoms but were exactly opposite in the way the atoms were arranged. The difference accounted for the different ways the crystals affected light. His discovery of these mirror-image molecules immediately established his scientific reputation.

Professor. In 1848, soon after his first discovery, Pasteur fulfilled his childhood dream by becoming a professor of chemistry at the University of Strasbourg. The following year, he married a young woman named Marie Laurent, the daughter of a university official. The couple would have five children. Only two survived into adulthood: a son, Jean-Baptiste, and a daughter, Marie-Louise. Marie-Louise Pasteur later married Rene Vallery-Radot, who wrote the first biography of his famous father-in-law.

▲ A nineteenth-century wood engraving of Pasteur in his laboratory; finding that his job at the École Normale left Pasteur too little time to do his experiments, Napoleon III agreed to help establish a special laboratory for him.

Participation: Development of Germ Theory

Request. Meanwhile, Pasteur continued his work on mirror-image molecules, making further breakthroughs. He discovered that, in general, only organic molecules (molecules produced by living organisms) changed the direction of polarized light. Tartaric acid was one such compound. Chemically produced versions of these molecules, Pasteur found, generally did not affect polarized light.

In 1854 the Pasteurs moved to Lille in northern France, where Louis had been offered a teaching post at the university. Shortly after arriving at Lille, Pasteur received a request from a local factory owner, a man named Bigo. Bigo's factory used fermentation to produce alcohol from beet juice. Hearing of Pasteur's familiarity with tartaric acid, Bigo asked him to help with some problems he was having with the fermentation process. This chance inquiry led to Pasteur's first interest in fermentation, and thus to his first steps toward germ theory.

Fermentation. One of the first things Pasteur did with the beet juice was to put samples of the fermenting liquid under a microscope. Like others who had done so, he saw small bits of yeast floating in it. At the time, fermentation—what happens when the sugar in a substance is changed into something else, such as alcohol—was thought to be a chemical process. That is, scientists believed that when, for example, grape juice changes into wine, its sugar molecules split themselves into simpler alcohol molecules in the same way that other chemical changes take place. Pasteur's first clue to a different view of fermentation came when he found that the beet juice alcohol changed the direction of polarized light. According to his earlier conclusions, that meant that it was organic. Something in the liquid was alive.

When others had identified the yeast in fermenting liquids, they had thought that perhaps it was responsible for the chemical changes. They thought it was a catalyst, a nonliving substance that causes chemical change. After much observation, Pasteur agreed that yeast caused fermentation. Careful experiments, however, persuaded him that it was not a catalyst at all. Yeast, he concluded, was a living organism. (Yeast is actually a single-celled fungus that behaves somewhat like bacteria.) It consumed the sugar, and alcohol was its waste product. He went on to demonstrate that other microorganisms, bacteria in this case, cause milk to go sour by fermenting sugar into lactic acid.

Microbiology. In 1857, while pursuing his experiments with fermentation, Pasteur was named director of Scientific Studies at his former school, the École Normale Supérieure in Paris. Soon afterward, he published his revolutionary findings in a short scientific paper. The paper is considered by his recent biographer, the scientist Rene J. Dubos, as "the beginning of scientific microbiology" (Dubos, p. 35). It was the first time that a real understanding of microscopic organisms had been achieved through experiments.

In the same paper Pasteur mentioned the possibility that his ideas about fermentation might somehow be applied to the problem of infectious diseases (diseases that can be spread). He had no real evidence yet, but in making the suggestion he revealed that he did have more ideas to test experimentally.

Silkworms. Pasteur firmly believed in applying the lessons of science to the practical problems of industry. In 1865 representatives of the silk industry approached him. The silkworms on which the industry relied had been attacked by a mysterious disease. Its rapid spread threatened the whole of French silk production. Pasteur accepted the challenge, though he knew nothing about silkworms. For five years, Pasteur worked on silkworm diseases, along with his other experiments. He found two separate diseases at work, one caused by a microscopic parasite, the other by bad nutrition. He figured out not only the diseases, but also how best to fight them. The silk industry was very important to the French economy at the time, and by saving it Pasteur won his first real fame. He also became known for strongly and publicly defending his views against those who disagreed with him.

Stroke. Finding that his job at the École Normale left him too little time to do his experiments, Pasteur resigned in 1867. Napoleon III, the French emperor, agreed to help establish a special laboratory for him at the École. The following year, Pasteur suffered a stroke that nearly killed him, leaving his left arm and leg permanently paralyzed. A few years earlier, his father and his two-year-old daughter Camille had died; shortly after that, his daughter Cecile, twelve, had died of typhoid fever. Yet it was during this time of deep suffering that Pasteur accomplished some of his greatest work.

Spontaneous generation. Aside from detecting silkworm diseases, during this period Pasteur also showed that germs in the air cause food or other substances to rot. Until then, some scientists believed that bacteria arose by themselves, for example in dead animals or plants. This theory was called spontaneous generation. Others disagreed, creating a major controversy in the scientific world. Pasteur had noticed how exposure to the air made some liquids ferment, or grow yeasts or bacteria, more quickly.

Pasteur designed specific experiments to determine whether it was something invisible in the air that was causing the fermentation, rather than it being caused by spontaneous generation within the liquid alone. Through these experiments, in which he placed bacteria-prone broths in special swan-necked vessels that could block out air, Pasteur was able to demonstrate that bacteria would only grow when air was allowed to pass through the vessel's neck, thus showing that it was invisible germs in the air, and not spontaneous generation, that were causing the growth of bacteria in the liquids. As a further experiment, he also subjected the unfermented liquids to the pure mountain air of the high Alps. No new bacteria grew in the germ-free environment.

Anthrax. Wine, silkworms, dead plants and animals—from these separate pieces Pasteur's genius was slowly putting together the jigsaw puzzle of his germ theory. During the 1870s, as his fame grew, Pasteur began work on the part of the puzzle that included human diseases. He first tackled anthrax, an animal disease that could be spread to humans. Building on discoveries made by the German scientist Robert Koch (sometimes called the cofounder of microbiology), Pasteur succeeded in developing a vaccination that protected animals against anthrax. Like silk, livestock were vitally important to the economy. In a public test, amid world attention, Pasteur infected sixty sheep, goats, and cows with anthrax. He had vaccinated thirty-one; twenty-nine were unprotected. Within a few days, all but four unprotected animals (the cows) were dead, and the four cows were badly ill. None of the vaccinated animals showed the slightest sign of illness. Pasteur had won a dramatic victory.

Rabies. His next success, however, was the one that won him widespread acclaim. Thousands of people died every year from rabies, a fatal disease contracted from the bite of an infected animal. After experiments failed to show any bacteria at work in

---

Pasteurization

If most of the germs are killed and others are kept out, a food can be made to last longer. Pasteur invented just such a process, now called pasteurization. He discovered that heating milk, for example, to a certain temperature for a certain amount of time kills most of the bacteria present in it. Today, dairies all over the world use pasteurization. It works for other foods also, especially liquids. Pasteur himself developed pasteurization techniques for wine and beer.

rabid animals, Pasteur realized that another kind of germ was the cause, a germ (later called a virus) too small to be detected by the microscopes of the day. After much work, Pasteur succeeded in creating a vaccine. It worked on animals, but Pasteur was unwilling to risk experimenting on humans.

Finally, in 1885 a boy named Joseph Meister, who had been bitten by a rabid dog, was brought to him. Rabies takes several weeks to show its effects, so the vaccine has time to take effect after the bite. Knowing that the boy would die without it, Pasteur injected him with the vaccine, continuing the injections over several days. The boy remained perfectly healthy. When he grew up, he became the gatekeeper at the Pasteur Institute in Paris. His devotion to Pasteur was dramatically illustrated when, in 1940, invading Germans ordered him to open Pasteur's grave site. Rather than do so, Meister committed suicide.

Aftermath

Pasteur Institute. The Pasteur Institute was opened in 1888, originally to promote research on rabies. Pasteur ran the institute until his death on September 28, 1895. The institute has since grown into a world center for research on infectious diseases, with thousands of employees at sites throughout France. It leads the way on AIDS research, for example, sharing credit for discovering the virus that causes the disease. Many of its scientists have won Nobel Prizes for their work.

For More Information

Dubos, Rene J. *Pasteur and Modern Science.* Madison, Wisconsin: Science Tech Publishers, 1988.

Dubos, Rene J. *Louis Pasteur: Free Lance Science.* New York: Scribners, 1976.

Latour, Bruno. *The Pasteurization of France.* New York: HUP, 1988.

Vallary-Rodot, Pasteur. *Louis Pasteur: A Great Life in Brief.* Translated by Alfred Joseph. New York: Knopf, 1958.

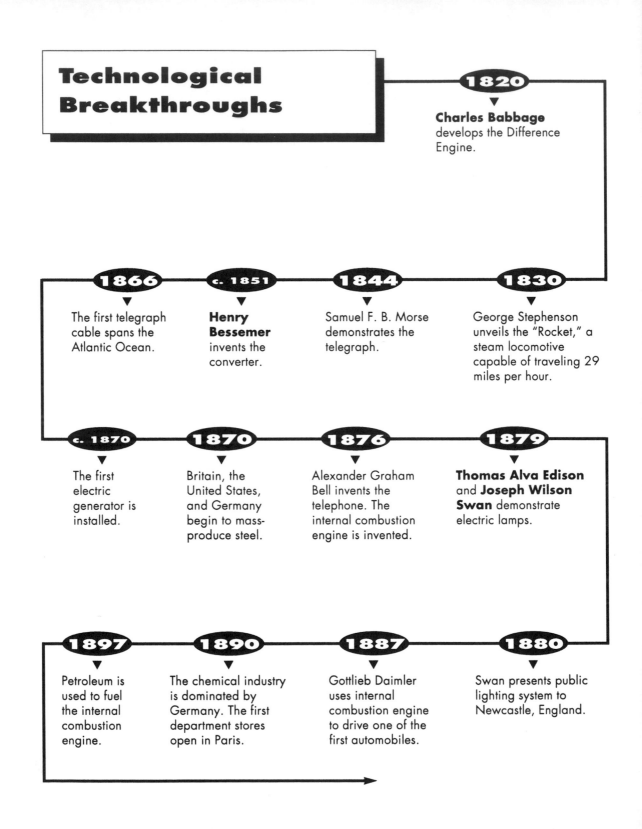

Technological Breakthroughs

1820
▼
Charles Babbage develops the Difference Engine.

1830
▼
George Stephenson unveils the "Rocket," a steam locomotive capable of traveling 29 miles per hour.

1844
▼
Samuel F. B. Morse demonstrates the telegraph.

c. 1851
▼
Henry Bessemer invents the converter.

1866
▼
The first telegraph cable spans the Atlantic Ocean.

c. 1870
▼
The first electric generator is installed.

1870
▼
Britain, the United States, and Germany begin to mass-produce steel.

1876
▼
Alexander Graham Bell invents the telephone. The internal combustion engine is invented.

1879
▼
Thomas Alva Edison and **Joseph Wilson Swan** demonstrate electric lamps.

1880
▼
Swan presents public lighting system to Newcastle, England.

1887
▼
Gottlieb Daimler uses internal combustion engine to drive one of the first automobiles.

1890
▼
The chemical industry is dominated by Germany. The first department stores open in Paris.

1897
▼
Petroleum is used to fuel the internal combustion engine.

TECHNOLOGICAL BREAKTHROUGHS

The last part of the eighteenth century and the beginning of the nineteenth were marked by an industrial revolution. Fueled to a large extent by British expansion into world markets, this first modern "revolution" in industry brought increases in textile production, the development of railroads, and demands for iron and coal. There was a flurry of excitement about new sources of energy and about machines to make the work of the new factory system more efficient. Toward the end of this period, **Charles Babbage** began to design machines that would perform the tiresome mathematical work that accompanied the rapidly expanding production facilities.

The second industrial revolution. Then in the last quarter of the nineteenth century, a new revolution took place, this time focusing on the materials of production—steel for rails, chemicals, and new uses for petroleum. Electricity, a bright new energy source that promised cleaner, more effective energy supplies for the burgeoning factories, inspired countless experiments and designs for its use. Britain, now thoroughly settled into factory production, led the other nations in a flood of manufacturing innovations.

England's textile mills were booming, creating a demand for more and more effective dyes and efficient means of transporting goods to markets. The British took a dim view of the use of highways to move their textile goods and looked to the development of its rail system. Steel, more malleable than iron, became a leading product, largely because of the continued work and inventiveness of men such as **Henry Bessemer.** Bessemer invented a machine that converted iron into steel efficiently. Soon the advantages of steel spread throughout Europe and across the ocean to the American colonies. Before the end of the century, both the United States and Germany were out-producing Britain in the production of the valuable metal.

Petroleum. Meanwhile, a new energy source, petroleum, began to find its way from simple gas lights into more industrial uses. Inventors throughout Europe and America began to search for ways to harness this new energy. These inventors found ways to produce internal combustion engines that ignited petroleum products in cylinders that could be made to drive the heaviest of equipment. Soon petroleum was put to use driving factory engines, then locomotives and ships, and finally the newest advance in highway transportation—the automobile.

Electricity. At the same time, experimenters were making progress in harnessing electricity. Electric motors began to drive some industrial machinery. Electricity also provided new sources of light and advances in communication. Samuel Morse was given credit for developing the telegraph; Alexander Graham Bell, the telephone; **Thomas Alva Edison,** the phonograph. The last half of the nineteenth century brought such new discoveries as the photograph and motion pictures. One obscure inventor, Elijah McCoy, focused on ways to use petroleum and graphite to lubricate machines while they were working. On this problem alone, McCoy took out more than fifty patents. Edison, working at his industrial research plant at Menlo Park, New Jersey, claimed the patent rights on a new invention each month. Inventions came so rapidly that it was nearly impossible to credit a single person with each new development. The pace of discovery was so fast, in fact, that it is difficult if not impossible to identify the first inventor of many innovations, for example, the automobile or the electric light.

A self-feeding revolution. The revolution fueled itself. Steel made it easier to transport goods, and British sea merchants took advantage of new ships to transport goods throughout the world. Factories grew to supply these markets, increasing the demand for labor. The wages of the new factory labor force grew with the demand for workers. Marketers searched for new ways to reach these more prosperous workers, and in the last decade of the century invented the department store, the first of which opened in Paris. Meanwhile, businessmen searched for ways to capture more of the growing markets. Many small industrialists were gobbled up by larger ones, which further fueled the revolution.

Edison and Swan. The invention of a working and reliable electric light is a fine example of the frenzy of invention in the late nineteenth century. Seemingly without knowledge of one another, two men, one British and one American, began to follow up on earlier efforts to use electricity to produce reliable light. Both eventually fixed on carbon as the resistor that would give bright and long-lasting light. By 1879 both men, **Joseph Wilson Swan** in Britain and Edison in America, were prepared to demonstrate very similar electric lights. Both were recognized inventors in other fields, and both had visions of lighting cities with their new lamps. Both were successful, and this success eventually brought them together—at first as opponents in courts and then as partners in one of the first electric light companies.

The first industrial revolution centered on textiles; the second one expanded into transportation, communication, and the development of entirely new products—all made possible by the discovery of the two new energy sources, petroleum and electricity. The fury of discovery led to perhaps the most important of all the nineteenth-century inventions: the industrial laboratory where the search for new tools and new products could be carried out independently of problems of manufacturing and marketing.

Charles Babbage

1792-1871

Personal Background

Family. The Babbage family was wealthy. Father Benjamin was a London banker and landowner. Mother Betty Plumleigh (Teape) was a member of a prosperous and respected Devonshire family. Benjamin and Betty had several children, only two of whom lived beyond infancy—one daughter and a son, Charles.

Charles Babbage was born at Totnes, in Devonshire, a county in southwest England, in 1792. A frail infant, Charles nevertheless proved to be very bright. He did well, or reasonably so, at Alphington and King Edwards Grammar School before spending three years in preparation for college at Enfield Academy. The boy's frailty often put him in great pain, but he discovered very early that he could endure the pain more easily by choosing some object or activity and totally concentrating on that subject instead of the pain. The power to concentrate was to become an important skill that he would draw upon throughout his life.

When he was eleven Babbage was sent to study with a clergyman at Alphington, where, his parents hoped, the clearer air would give him strength. The instructions were that he was to relax and his studies not be made too taxing. Babbage, therefore, had a great deal of idle time, which he used to devise experiments and question old ideas. One idea he remembered testing was the popular notion that Satan would appear to try to tempt people

▲ Charles Babbage

Event: Beginning the development of calculating machines.

Role: A brilliant student of mathematics, Charles Babbage spent most of his life in a futile attempt to create machines for calculating mathematical and astronomical tables. His plans for such calculators, which he called the "Difference Engine" and the "Analytical Engine," although never fully realized, are regarded as important initial groundwork for the later development of computers.

away from prayer. The test the boy devised was to lock himself in an unused attic, draw a circle of blood on the floor, stand within it, and recite the Lord's Prayer. No sign of Satan appeared, but the experience left Babbage, who was not always very brave, nervous about noises and about the Lord's Prayer for days.

From the beginning, school was not very challenging to young Babbage. He found that he had plenty of time for playing pranks on his classmates and joining them in events not approved of by the school—like the time he and some other boys brought vodka into the school, mixed it with liqueur and held a party, soon finding themselves in no shape to attend the school's religious service. In his later school years, Babbage was fond of forming clubs for purposes of nonsense. There was, for example, a college Ghost Club and an Extractor's Club.

College. Babbage grew to be a handsome, fun-loving, and energetic young man. He had many friends; some of them met regularly for Sunday breakfast. He was also known to entertain his friends at parties of two or three hundred people. But mathematics was an early favorite subject that held Babbage's interest all his life.

A Rule of the Extractor's Club

Members of this club agreed to keep others up-to-date on their living quarters. If one failed to give the club an address within a year, that member was to be considered to have been shut up in an insane asylum. Members were sworn to make every effort to secure the errant club member's release from his madhouse.

When he was nineteen, Babbage entered Trinity College at Cambridge and, three years later, graduated from another Cambridge college, Peterhouse. The change of colleges revealed another quality in Babbage—he was very competitive. He had established firm friendships at Trinity with John Hershel and George Peacock, both also excellent mathematics students, and Babbage feared that at the same school he might come in third in the graduation rankings. He wanted to be at the top of his class, and so he moved in his last college year to make sure that happened, though it was not as if college were particularly challenging to any of the three.

On his way to college in 1811, Babbage had purchased a book by the French mathematician Sylvestre Lacroix, an explanation of calculus that was more up-to-date than that of the more famous

English physicist and mathematician, Isaac Newton. This he pored over as if it were his favorite novel. Then at college he decided that English mathematics, dominated by the notation system and ideas of Isaac Newton, was far behind the mathematical work in France. To encourage mathematics education in England, he and his two friends, Herschel and Peacock, decided to translate Lacroix's work into English. Babbage was also interested in logarithms. As he was concentrating on some tables of logarithms one evening, a friend asked him what he was thinking about. "I am thinking that all these tables might be calculated by machinery" (Moseley, p. 48). It would be ten years before he would begin to build such a machine.

Participation: Beginning the Development of Calculating Machines

By the time he graduated from college, Babbage was thinking about machines that could carry out the mathematics involved in astronomical calculations. No accurate and speedy method of making calculations by machine then existed— only simple tools like the abacus and Napier's bones, a set of graduated rods used to perform multiplication quickly.

The Difference Engine. By 1820 Babbage had made progress in developing a machine that would calculate more exact values for such mathematical necessities as tables of logarithms, sines, and cosines. He was convinced that such a machine was necessary by his discovery

Teaching Mathematics

From 1828 to 1839 Babbage was a professor of mathematics at Cambridge. It is one of the oddities of his life that, even though he had been a champion of improving English education, he is not known to have ever even taught a class while he was a professor.

of the many inaccuracies that existed in the astronomical tables used in England at that time. If only the necessary calculations could be done by an automatic machine, and the results printed out automatically, these tables could be made more accurate and science could advance more rapidly. Drawing hundreds of plans and hiring mechanics to help him, he began to build a model of a machine he called the Difference Engine. In 1823 the Royal Society approved of his work, and the British government decided to help build such an engine by providing some of the money.

▲ A portion of Babbage's Difference Engine built between 1823 and 1833; although his plans for calculators were never fully realized, Babbage laid the initial groundwork for the later development of computers.

Although the plans seemed, on the whole, good, progress was slow. Babbage hired the best mechanics and engineers to help with the construction, but after five years of work, the machine was still not finished. For one thing, instrument-making was not yet refined enough to make the hundreds of exact rods and gear wheels needed. For another, Babbage, like many other brilliant men, could not contain himself to concentrate all his efforts on one activity. It did not help matters that he was constantly altering the plans and making improvements while the mechanics were trying to work.

Then, too, there were street musicians who would play in the streets near his apartment at night, disturbing his concentration. The more he fought with them, the more they would gather under his window to pester him. Babbage was changing rapidly from a happy-go-lucky youth to a crotchety old man.

Exhausted from feuding with musicians, the government, and the Royal Society (he had become a member in 1826), Babbage was persuaded to visit continental Europe in 1827 and 1828. There he studied Europe's most advanced production facilities and met with many of the learned men of his day. Although the working holiday did not give him any ideas about getting government support or working with British scientists, he did bring back many ideas for improving British industry. Some of these he published in a very influential book, *On the Economy of Manufactures and Machinery*.

The Analytic Engine. Back at work, Babbage found that his chief mechanic had quit, taking with him special tools designed for the project and many of the plans. This man, Joseph Clement, claimed that he was owed £7,000, a large sum of money at that time, and apparently he was correct. Neither Babbage nor the British government disputed his actions. It didn't matter so much, however, because by this time Babbage had decided that he wanted to make a calculating machine with much greater capability. This machine would be able to begin a problem and then branch out to examine several different alternatives to its solution. In addition, the machine would be able to perform one

> ## Disaster and Despair
>
> The year 1827 marked the lowest point in Babbage's life. In June 1814 he had married Georgiana Whitmore. Although he rarely seemed to pay much attention to her, the two were deeply in love. Over the next thirteen years, Georgiana bore eight Babbage children. Four died in infancy, and a favorite daughter died in her teens. Only three sons survived. In the single year of 1827, Babbage's wife, two children, and his father all died. Those deaths, along with the failure to complete his machine, led Babbage to a near nervous breakdown and to his extended trip to Europe.

mathematical operation after another following instructions given it by cards punched to allow fine steel wires to operate switches at the correct times. Some of these ideas were used in modern computing, but in Babbage's day, few understood what the machine would do, and even fewer could see why such a machine was needed. The daughter of the poet Lord Byron understood, and she, Lady Lovelace, encouraged Babbage, planned problems for the machine, and reviewed the inventor's calculations. Lady Lovelace has been called the world's first computer programmer.

Babbage had angered the Royal Society by insisting that the mathematical notations of Gottfried Leibniz were easier to work with than those of the Englishman Isaac Newton. Babbage's irritation had grown to such a point that he had, at one time, suggested that the Royal Society itself was a block to increased knowledge and should be abandoned. So when he proposed to build the Analytical Engine, there was little support from the philosophers and scientists. And there was no one in government who understood. Government officials who reviewed a proposal for financing sometimes could not even understand whether the requests were for money to finish the Difference Engine or to build the new Analytical Engine. The result was that although Babbage continued to work on the ideas at least until the mid-1850s, neither machine was ever finished in England. It was not until after his death that mathematicians began to appreciate the advanced thinking represented by the Babbage "computers."

Aftermath

Accomplishments. Babbage did not live to see his dream fulfilled of an analytical machine capable of rapid and accurate constructions of necessary mathematics and astronomic tables. He did, however, introduce many important ideas into British science and industry. When he was about forty, he had constructed a table of logarithms of much greater accuracy than any then in use. He developed a new branch of the mathematics of analysis. At one time, he became interested in efficient package delivery, which led him to investigate the postal system. He proposed a standard charge for delivering a letter, regardless of its destination. He also proposed that the English postal service begin delivering packages, thereby fathering the parcel post service. Babbage's interests also took him into the field of medicine, where he invented the ophthalmoscope. He had also contributed to rail travel by making detailed studies on how to make railcars more stable and easier to ride.

Writing. Babbage died having written and published more than eighty books and articles. He had published his log tables and followed them with a book of interesting mathematical problems and solutions. Most of his other writings were about mathematics. He also, however, left a lasting mark on British manufacturing and marketing and stirred British science with a book titled *Reflections on the Decline of Science in England and on Some of Its Causes*. In his last years, he wrote his autobiography, titled *Passages from the Life of a Philosopher.*

Death. On October 18, 1871, Babbage died after a lingering illness. Few paid attention to his death, although he himself had been thinking about it for some time. He had said that he did not want to die but would gladly do so if he could come back for three days five hundred years later (Moseley, p. 258). Even in his old age, Babbage remained curious and interested in human progress.

After Babbage's death, Babbage's son Henry carried on the interests of his father. Henry, who had a distinguished military career, also became a spokesman for his father's accomplishments.

> ## It Worked!
>
> Babbage had put much of his effort into fighting science and government. But in Sweden, an engineer named Georg Scheutz picked up a magazine article that described the Difference Engine. Working from that article, Scheutz made a perfectly workable machine—although not of the mathematical precision that Babbage dreamed. Scheutz completed his machine while Babbage was still struggling and squabbling.

For More Information

Campbell, Kelley Martin, editor. *The Works of Charles Babbage.* New York: New York University Press, 1988.

Moseley, Maboth. *Irascible Genius: The Life of Charles Babbage.* Chicago: Henry Regnery, 1964.

Thomas, Shirley. *Computers: Their History, Present Applications, and Future.* New York: Holt, Rinehart and Winston, 1965.

Henry Bessemer

1813-1898

Personal Background

Early life. Perhaps few people in history have had their path in life so clearly marked at such an early age as Henry Bessemer, and even fewer have taken that path as easily. His father was a French inventor and engraver who had migrated to Charlton in southeast England. There he had established a type factory, in which Henry was to receive his early education.

Henry Bessemer was born on January 19, 1813, in Charlton, where, almost from birth, he seemed destined to become an inventor and metal worker. The boy spent many hours in his father's foundry learning about metals and how to shape them. The young Bessemer seemed always to be modeling or designing machinery and painting. By the time he was eighteen, he had learned enough at the foundry to strike out on his own. He had grown to adulthood with a reputation for being careful, imaginative, and determined to accomplish what he set out to do. With that temperament, he soon found employment as a model-maker and designer in London factories, while spending time on his own trying to invent improvements to existing machines.

First patented invention. One of his first inventions was immediately accepted by the British government. At the time, Britain was plagued with forged documents. The government offices had stamped such important papers as deeds to identify

▲ **Henry Bessemer**

Event: Producing steel economically.

Role: Henry Bessemer invented a machine called the converter, for changing pig iron to "malleable iron," or steel. His inventions greatly reduced the cost of producing steel and made it possible to shape items such as rails for the growing mechanized industries.

them as legal, and these stamps were easily copied. Bessemer invented a machine that would press the stamp into the document, making it more difficult to forge. The British government was so impressed that it immediately adopted the new machine for its offices.

Crimean War. Bessemer's next invention was an improved method for making bronze powder, then a widely used metal. This development was a financial success and allowed Bessemer to establish his own brass foundry in London. He was just in time for the Crimean War (1853). Russia and Turkey took to the battlefields over a Russian claim to be the protector of Christians on some Turkish land. France and Britain were offended by the high-handedness of Russia's emperor Nicholas I and were more than willing to help Turkey in this battle. As battles wore on, the need for better weapons and missiles grew. Bessemer's foundry was caught up in the manufacture of missiles for the cannons of Britain and France. It was this work that led to the discovery for which Bessemer is best known—a low-cost way to make steel.

Bessemer's Reward

Although the British government accepted Bessemer's stamp and used it everywhere, Bessemer gained little from the invention and received no recognition for his work. Many years later, when he was much more famous, he would call this to the attention of British royalty. By way of an apology, Queen Victoria knighted the aging inventor, making him Sir Henry Bessemer.

The inventor devised a cannon shell that would revolve as it passed through the cannon to its target. The revolving shell could travel faster and more accurately than the old cannon balls. Unfortunately, cannons of that day were made of brittle cast iron and could not stand the extra pressure of the spinning shell, so Bessemer's invention had no effect on the war. It did, however, affect the French ruler Louis Napoléon, who invited the inventor to work for him. For several years, Bessemer worked to improve French armaments.

Participation: Producing Steel Economically

The need for iron and steel. Brass was not sturdy enough for some of the tasks performed in the new factories of the Industrial Revolution. Iron was much more useful, but producing good iron required a great deal of energy. In the early nineteenth century, six-and-one-half tons of coke or coal were needed to make one ton of iron. In addition, iron was made in crucibles, heat-tolerant containers that could handle only a small amount of ore at one time. The new machinery of the weaving mills demanded more and more good iron—iron that could be hammered to make the wheels and cams of the machines. In 1850 all of Britain produced only sixty tons of iron a year. In his bronze foundry, Bessemer began to experiment with iron.

Steel-making. The demand for tool parts had encouraged a great deal of interest in making a form of iron that could be pressed and molded into the required shapes. This had led to the discovery of the special qualities of steel—its toughness and malleability. By 1744 Benjamin Huntsman had produced hardened steel at temperatures of nine hundred degrees Centigrade. By 1849 the famous Krupp factory in Germany had succeeded in making a steel cannon. Still, the use of steel and refined iron was not commercially profitable for most needs. In 1851 an American named William Kelley produced steel by blasting air through molten pig iron. But, as is often the case, credit for a great invention went not to the inventor but to the person who first made the invention profitable. In this case, the profiteer was Henry Bessemer.

There is no actual evidence that Bessemer knew of the discovery made by Kelley, but soon after Kelley introduced his idea, Bessemer announced that he had developed a way to make steel cheaply. A preheated blast of air through the molten iron resulted in steel that could be rolled on giant rollers. It may have been Kelley's idea first, but Bessemer knew what to do with it. Self-confident and eager to press for new wealth and glory, Bessemer designed a great crucible in the form of a giant jug in which iron and other ingredients could be placed and forced to interact by great heat and by the blowing up of warm air from the bottom through the melting

> ## Bessemer the Inventor
>
> Bessemer's third invention was an improvement over the old hand-typesetting. Sitting at a large frame with a keyboard similar to that of a piano, one woman could stamp out nearly six thousand letters an hour while another woman sat nearby and arranged the letters in lines inside a wooden box. This Pianotype machine was hailed as a great printing help, but it had its detractors. Women were not supposed to do heavy and exacting work like typesetting, so the men of the printing industry looked on the Pianotype with suspicion.

batch inside. Called a "converter," this machine could handle tons of material at a time and could produce the extraordinarily useful steel at an unheard-of speed.

Almost immediately, Bessemer took the time to let the world know about his discovery and invention. In 1856 he read a paper to the British Association for the Advancement of Science about the "Manufacture of Malleable Iron and Steel without Fuel." Of course, his converter still needed fuel, but now a few hundred pounds of coke would do what six or seven tons of fuel had done earlier. He was immediately famous. His converter was widely adopted, and Bessemer grew wealthy.

For much of the rest of his life, Bessemer would continue to make improvements on his converter. One improvement was to turn the giant melting machine on its side so that air could be blasted into the mix while heat was applied from the top. With each invention, the Bessemer converter improved so that by 1860, Bessemer could produce twenty-five tons of steel from pig iron in just twenty-five minutes. Now steel could be produced so cheaply that it could be used in such things as railway rails. In addition, producing rails was now really practical because they could be rolled and pressed into shape without the endless hammering of the forger.

Most likely, Bessemer did not "invent" steel-making. But he created the tools that increased the efficiency of the steel-making process, thus greatly accelerating the Industrial Revolution. This was particularly true in America, where advances in iron and steel-making had already expanded, and in Britain, where the demand for transportation exploded with the invention of power-driven spinning and weaving machines, which were turning out products that needed to be moved to market. Britain had opposed experiments to make trucks and vans for road transportation, and the empire had turned to rails as the best means of transporting the new goods.

Bessemer the publicist. Bessemer continued to invent and improve his steel-making. But he took time to let the world know that he was the leader in this technology. In 1865 he presented a paper titled "On the Manufacture of Cast Steel, Its Purposes and

Employment as a Substitute for Wrought Iron." By that time, he had already been recognized as one of England's great engineers, winning the Telford Medal in 1855 from the British Institute of Civil Engineers. Later he also received the Albert Medal from the Society of Arts. Along with these honors, Bessemer became quite wealthy.

Aftermath

The constant inventor. Bessemer continued to experiment and invent far into his old age. He patented an invention for forcing molten metals into molds. He developed improvements in methods for embossing and printing. He even worked out a way to emboss velvet. But it was his last invention that finally resulted in perhaps his first total failure.

The level cabin. For Bessemer, every experience seemed to stimulate an idea for experiment. Ships in the late nineteenth century were subject to the whims of the weather. There were no stabilizers as there are now to keep ships from rolling; life in a ship's cabin, no matter how well it was equipped, was hard. In his later years, Bessemer set out to invent a ship's cabin mounted to the deck in such a way that it would remain level throughout any weather. He did produce such a cabin, but its design fell short. The "level cabin" was so uncertain and so expensive that it never found its way to market.

Bessemer died in London on May 15, 1898, still attempting to make new creations and improve the old.

For More Information

Ashton, T. S. *Iron and Steel in the Industrial Revolution.* 2nd ed. Manchester: Manchester University Press, 1951.

Burn, Duncan. *The Economic History of Steelmaking, 1867-1939.* Cambridge, England: Cambridge University Press, 1961.

Derry, T. K., and Trevor L. Williams. *A Short History of Technology.* New York: Oxford University Press, 1961.

Sisco, A., and C. S. Smith. *Memoirs on Steel and Iron.* Chicago: University of Chicago Press, 1956.

Joseph Wilson Swan

1828-1914

Personal Background

Early life. Joseph Wilson Swan was born on October 31, 1828, in Sunderland, northern England, to parents who seem to have decided early that their son should have the freedom to find a career for himself. As a very young boy, they allowed Swan to roam freely about the community and inquire into anything that interested him. He could and did investigate most of the industries in Sunderland, as well as the activities of the port and the goings-on in the public buildings.

Still, Swan's parents were intent that he be educated for some profession. He was enrolled first in a "dame school," a sort of home school run by three old ladies. From there he was placed in a private school taught by a minister, Dr. Wood. Later, when he was old enough, Swan was taken on as an apprentice in a small chemical company run by two partners. Apprentices normally were signed on until they learned the craft or for a number of years, often seven. Whatever the arrangement with Swan, the two owners died before he could complete his apprenticeship, but not before he had learned a great deal about chemistry.

Since the company no longer existed, Swan was free of his apprenticeship obligations. He was, however, now committed to working as a chemist. His brother-in-law, John Mawson, had his own chemical company in nearby Newcastle-upon-Tyne, and

▲ **Joseph Wilson Swan**

Event: Developing the electric light.

Role: Following nearly the same path as Thomas Alva Edison in America, British inventor Joseph Wilson Swan began to experiment with filaments that would heat to a white heat as electricity was introduced, but would not burn up. Almost simultaneously, the two inventors introduced the electric light in grand demonstrations in London and New York.

Swan joined his company. At the same time, he continued his outside education by attending lectures and reading as many books as possible about science and inventions. The reading led him to two dominant interests: he studied photography and read about the earlier efforts of J. W. Starr and W. E. Staite to use electricity for lighting.

In 1845 Swan had the opportunity to attend a lecture by Staite. That already famous experimenter told of his efforts to use electrical resistance to create light. Swan began to think about materials that might make a filament that would get white hot but not burn up when electricity was passed through it. Within three years after this lecture, Swan was deeply involved in experimenting with ways to make an electric light.

Joseph Swan's Inventive Mind

While he experimented with electric lighting and worked as a chemist, Swan made several other important discoveries. He developed a photographic plate of glass coated with gelatin flaked with carbon and potassium dichromate. When this plate was exposed to light, some of the gelatin became insoluble in water. The remaining material could be dissolved in water and washed off to leave a photograph. The trouble was that the surface of the gelatin also refused to dissolve. Swan overcame this problem by pasting a sheet of paper to the gelatin surface then scraping the whole material off the glass plate. A refinement of his method is still used to develop black and white film. Swan also developed bromine print paper for photographs still used in the 1990s.

Participation: Developing the Electric Light

History of the light. Having read as much as he could about science experiments, Swan knew that Staite was not the first to think of using electricity to produce light. As early as 1810 Sir Humphry Davy had demonstrated an electric arc and experimented with platinum filaments (threads) in search of something that would give light without burning. Most of the attention after that had gone toward developing an arc lamp, an arrangement of electric conductors that would give light by making a strong arc between two connectors. In 1845, however, a man by the name of Starr had taken out a patent for an electric light—which apparently didn't work well since nothing ever came of the patent. Swan did not want to waste his own time repeating earlier experiments. Early on he decided that a proper filament could be made from carbon. The problem was how to prepare a carbon thread and under what conditions to try to light it.

Carbon threads and electric lights. In 1848, while supporting himself by working as a chemist for a photography firm, Swan began to experiment with making carbon threads for filaments in a lamp. His experiments were straightforward and involved cooking strips of paper to make carbon thread. But carbon produced in this way did not hold together. It was necessary to cook the paper with something that would make it stick together enough to conduct some electricity. Swan experimented with all kinds of additives to the paper strips—including an oil derived from tar, which produced an unsavory mess.

Vacuum tubes. Finally, Swan produced a sturdy carbon filament that could be inserted in an electric circuit and would light up momentarily. The early attempts lasted only for split seconds. What was needed was a glass tube into which the filament could be inserted and air pumped out. When Swan experimented with a vacuum tube, his filaments lasted longer, but vacuum pumps in the mid-nineteenth century were not very good. He was forced to continue experimenting until 1865, when another inventor, Herman Sprengel, developed a better vacuum pump.

Then Swan began working with a pump-maker by the name of Charles Stearn. Between the two of them, they produced a serviceable filament of carbon in a glass tube vacuumed well enough that the carbon would light up and not fall apart. They continued to improve this model, developing a way to vacuum the tube twice—once after its first use—to purge the air even more. Swan had produced a functional electric incandescent lamp.

Edison. Far off in America, **Thomas Alva Edison** (see entry) had taken another approach. He had developed the idea of an industrial research laboratory that would invent many items that Edison thought he could sell. The laboratory would throw as many capable workers into a project as were needed to complete the work in a reasonable amount of time. Sometime in the 1870s Edison turned the attention of his workers to the problem of the electric light. Apparently, Edison knew of the work of Sir Humphry Davy, too. He began by trying to make a platinum filament work. He went on to try many other possible filaments, and he could use his staff to conduct more trials in less time than it took Swan. Edison eventually found a way to make a practical electric light using carbon for the filament.

Introducing the electric incandescent lamp. In 1878 and 1879 Swan demonstrated his electric lamp, and in 1880 he began to manufacture lamps in a town near Sunderland. The later problems with Edison came because Swan had so little interest in protecting his invention that he did not immediately apply for a patent. Meanwhile, by 1879 Edison had produced an incandescent lamp, which he immediately patented. He established the Edison Electric Company to sell his product about the same time that Swan began selling lights in Britain. In 1882 Edison took Swan to court, claiming patent violation. His claim was soon disallowed, however, and the following year the two inventors joined to form the Edison and Swan United Electric Light Company, directed by Edison.

Who Really Invented the Electric Light?

A monument topped by a giant electric light still stands at the site of the original Menlo Park laboratory in New Jersey. It lauds Thomas Edison as the inventor of the light. But there are others who give the credit to Joseph Swan. Perhaps no one person deserves the credit. You be the judge:

1810	Sir Humphry Davy reports an arc between two electric poles.
1845	Starr takes out a British patent on an electric light.
1870	An arc lamp lights Dungeness Harbor in Kent, England.
1876	There are two exhibitions of lights at the United States Centennial Exposition.
1878	Paul Jablochkov demonstrates the "electric candle" in Paris.
1878	Charles F. Brush uses the arc light in Cleveland.

Aftermath

Other inventions. Joining with Edison to sell electric lights did not stop Swan's eagerness to explore other subjects. He went on to invent an electric safety lamp for miners, although it would be many years before the cost of such a lamp could be brought down to a practical level. Swan also invented a sealed lead-cell battery, which solved the problem of acid leaking from batteries. Then he tried to make a fuel cell.

In 1885 Swan demonstrated a way to make "artificial silk," much like rayon, by adding nitrate to cotton, dissolving the mess in acetic acid, and forcing it through a fine dye to make a thread. Nor was he finished with photography. Before he died, Swan had amassed seventy patents related to photographs and their preparation.

Honors. In 1884 Swan was elected to membership in the Royal Society, and in 1894 he was knighted by Queen Victoria. Swan was also awarded a medal for his photography work by the Royal Photographic Society.

The prolific British inventor of the incandescent light died at Warlingham in southeast England on May 27, 1914. He was eighty-five years old.

For More Information

Aldridge, Bill G., and others. *The Incandescent Lamp.* Pennsylvania: American Association of Physics, 1975.

Baldwin, Neil. *Edison: Inventing the Century.* New York: Hyperion, 1985.

Canby, Edward Tatnall. *A History of Electricity.* New York: Hawthorne, 1963.

Cox, James A. *A Century of Light.* New York: Benjamin, 1979.

Thomas Alva Edison

1847-1931

Personal Background

The Edison family. Thomas Alva Edison's great-grandfather John Edison chose to remain a British subject during the American Revolution, and he served as a spy for British general Richard Howe in New Jersey. With the British defeat, John became unpopular and was forced to flee to Canada in order to avoid execution. His grandson Sam also chose the losing side in a conflict when tensions broke out between British and French Canadians. He was force to move to Milan, Ohio, in 1837. It was there that Thomas Edison was born on February 11, 1847, the youngest of seven children in the Edison family.

Childhood. A photograph of Edison at the age of three pictures a chubby child with piercing eyes, looking straight ahead as if daring the photographer to do something. It suggests that he had inherited the family traits of independence, stubbornness, and self-confidence. By the time the family moved to Port Huron, Michigan, when Edison was seven years old, these qualities had already shown themselves in some of the boy's own experiments. Stories survive about the young boy sitting on some bird's eggs because he had learned that parent birds do that to help the young hatch. Another story tells of Edison setting fire to his father's barn just to see what would happen. It is no wonder that his father later remembered, "He did not share to any extent in the sports of his

▲ **Thomas Alva Edison**

Event: Developing the industrial research laboratory.

Role: Thomas Alva Edison was America's most prolific inventor, claiming an improved ticker tape machine, phonograph, and electric light among the many developments for which he, at his peak activity, received a new patent at the rate of one each month. His method of inventing resulted in even more additions to the world's tools. Edison was the first director of an industrial research laboratory.

neighborhood. He never knew real boyhood like the other boys" (Gies, p. 330). Edison was too busy thinking up new things to try.

Education. It was in Port Huron that Edison had his only formal education, though he was not much interested in it. He paid little attention to the teacher and drew on his slate, refusing to answer questions. When, after three months, his mother, Nancy, overheard one teacher suggest that he was exceptionally dumb, she decided to take matters into her own hands. Edison was taken out of school, and his mother, who had once been a schoolteacher, taught him herself. She was certain that her son was exceptional all right—exceptionally bright and bored with classrooms.

A Dangerous Experimenter
Among his many experiments as a very young boy, Edison is said to have tied two cats by the tails and rubbed their fur to generate electricity. He also mixed explosive chemicals in the family basement. The experiments resulted in his almost drowning in the town canal, being caught between an angry goat and a nest of bees, and nearly suffocating after falling into grain in a silo.

Even though there is some evidence that Edison was born with dyslexia, a problem that makes reading difficult, he did, under his mother's guidance, learn to read. By the age of twelve, he read and wrote well enough to get himself a job.

Newspaper career. It was 1859 and the Grand Trunk Railway was just opening a route from Port Huron to Detroit, a distance of about thirty miles. Businessmen and commuters could ride the train into Detroit in the morning and return to Port Huron that evening. The husky, bright-eyed Edison applied for a job selling candy and newspapers on the train rides between the two cities.

Edison caught the train at seven o'clock each morning to make the nearly three-hour trip, then worked on the train back to Port Huron beginning about six o'clock in the evening. The job allowed many hours of free time. On the train, Edison used this time to set up a chemistry laboratory in the baggage car—a laboratory that would eventually get him into trouble. Later, he managed to buy a printing press and print his own newspaper of local interest, the *Weekly Herald*. He was soon earning about $45 a month, most of which he spent on tools for his laboratory, which he equipped to handle experiments with electricity.

During the long layovers in Detroit, Edison discovered the new Detroit Public Library and began to read. He later claimed that he began with the first book on the lowest shelf and read all the books in the library. As unlikely as this seems, it would be in keeping with his character; Edison was beginning to be very thorough in everything he did. Sometime in his career as a newsboy on the train, Edison began to lose his hearing. His near deafness worsened during the rest of his life.

Telegrapher. On one trip, at a stop in one of the towns between Port Huron and Detroit, Edison was standing near the train when he saw a small child running near the tracks toward an oncoming train. He rescued the child who turned out to be the son of the station master. As a reward the station master offered to give Edison free training to become a telegrapher. For the following five years, he would be a telegraph sender and receiver, traveling wherever he could find a job—Stratford Junction in Ontario; Toledo, Ohio; Fort Wayne, Indiana; Indianapolis, Indiana; and when jobs were scarce, New Orleans, Louisiana, where he was tempted for a brief time to sail to Brazil in search of work. Always his first purchases from his paychecks were electrical gadgets or chemicals for his laboratory. His experiments led to some interesting inventions: an automatic clock that would allow him to be clocked in at the required regular intervals (and allow him to sleep); a gadget that would slow down messages registered by telegraph to make the work easier (they also led to his being fired in Louisville, Kentucky). The chemistry laboratory he created on the second floor of the train depot shook and spilled his supply of sulfuric acid, allowing it to seep through the floor and ruin the station master's desk below.

Participation: Developing the Industrial Research Laboratory

Influenced by reading. The reading habit he acquired at the Detroit Public Library began to shape what Edison really wanted to do. He had read Isaac Newton's *Principia* and decided that he never wanted to do anything that required so much mathematics. Later he read **Michael Faraday**'s *Experimental Researches in Electricity* and noticed that Faraday seemed to experiment without using mathematics much at all. Faraday became a model for Edison, who now decided to experiment with electrical inventions.

William's Electrical Shop. While in Boston in 1868 and 1869 Edison rented a corner of William's Electrical Shop on Court Street and began to experiment. He was very excited about his first invention—an electric machine that allowed legislators to cast aye and nay votes electronically. The machine worked very well. There was just one problem—nobody was interested in buying the gadget. Edison vowed never again to invent something no one wanted.

At that time, brokers everywhere were becoming fond of the ticker tape machine that rolled stock prices and exchanges almost continuously, printing them on a long tape. Edison's next adventure led to a greatly improved ticker tape machine. But Edison was not impressed. By that time he had also lost interest in Boston. He did not patent the machine. Still, his work in the corner of William's Electrical Shop had given him confidence to commit himself fully to working on his inventions.

New York. Edison now moved to New York, where he announced that he would work full time as an inventor. It was a bold announcement since he had no money. In fact, he was so broke that he had to borrow a dollar from a friend and make that do for food money for three days. Another friend arranged for him to sleep on the floor of the Gold Exchange, where Edison could see the ticker tapes rolling all day, and where a stroke of luck started him on the way to success. One day, the ticker tape machine broke and sent the people of the Exchange into a panic. Edison quickly found the problem and repaired the machine.

For this, Edison was hired by the Gold Indicator Company as assistant to the company's chief electrical engineer, Franklin Pope. He would earn a huge salary, $500 each month. Soon, however, Pope left to start his own company, and Edison took his place. He had not worked at Gold long before the company was gobbled up by Western Union. Edison left the job and joined

The Boston Test

As his last fling at telegraphy, Edison applied for a job as telegrapher in Boston and was given a test. He was to receive a message from New York. Other telegraphers in Boston had arranged to have that message sent by the fastest telegrapher there. But by this time, Edison had mastered his work. He took the message so easily that at one time he interrupted to tell the speedy sender to take a break and send the message with his other foot.

Franklin Pope in a new electrical company. The new company's first effort was to make an improved stock market ticker tape machine. It sold to Western Union for $15,000. Edison continued to make improvements on this machine until Western Union president Marshall Lefferts decided to buy the rights to all the changes. When Lefferts asked him what he wanted for all his rights, Edison wondered if he dared request $5,000. Finally, he thought it safer to ask Lefferts to suggest a price. The president of Western Union shocked him by offering $40,000. In addition, Edison was hired to manufacture the new machines for Western Union. It made possible what he had dreamed of—a plant devoted to invention and supported by manufacture.

Edison set up his first combination factory-laboratory in Newark, New Jersey. There his workmen made ticker tape machines and worked on inventions. Edison carefully hired the best available craftsmen, mechanics, and electrical engineers, and these workers followed his instructions in working on as many as forty-five inventions at a time. At the peak of the Newark factory's output, Edison took out a patent on new developments at the rate of one a month.

Honeymoon. In 1871 Edison married Mary Stilwell. The two would have a happy life together and raise three children before Mary died in 1884. But the beginning of the marriage was unusual. By that time, Edison had established his pattern of working almost constantly, allowing only for brief naps in the course of each day. His commitment to work did not allow him much time for a honeymoon. He and Mary were married and enjoyed a brief time together but, within an hour after the wedding, Edison was back to work.

Edison's method of experimenting was to try and try again. Every failure brought some new knowledge to help in the next attempt. Thus the company founded by Pope and Edison might make a hundred or a thousand attempts before hitting on the right solution to a problem.

Menlo Park. Finally the company that Edison now headed fell to the financial offer of a bigger company. It merged with the Automatic Telegraph Company. In 1873 a financial panic slowed sales of the products he manufactured, but Edison was now wealthy

▲ An 1878 photograph with Edison and one of his Menlo Park inventions, a phonograph.

enough and had such a strong reputation that he could really fulfill his dream. He would abandon manufacturing altogether and build a laboratory dedicated to creating marketable inventions.

Edison found a small town in New Jersey just six miles from Plainfield and only twenty-five miles from New York. It was called Menlo Park. There he had a two-story building constructed that looked very much like a large home or a church. The first floor contained a small office for Edison and a giant workshop, and behind it a machine shop. The second floor was all one very large laboratory. All the work spaces were filled with the most up-to-date tools available. These tools were used by the best machinists, mechanics, engineers, and inventors Edison could find. All worked long hours to make the laboratory a great industrial developer. One of his employees, John Ott, explained why they were all willing to work as long as Edison did: He "made me feel that I was making something WITH him, I wasn't just a workman" (Gies, p. 339). The number of employees at Menlo Park rose and fell as the number of projects changed. But so excited were the workers there that those laid off one week would often return the next to work even if they were not on the payroll. Edison always found a way to pay them.

A Few of the Inventions from Menlo Park
A recording (writing) telegraph
The carbon telephone
An electric pen
The phonograph
The Jeannette—the first electric dynamo
The phonometer—a voice transmitter
The tasimeter—to measure the sun's heat
A dictating machine
The motion picture camera and projector
A cement kiln

From 1875 to 1892 the house of invention at Menlo Park turned out an amazing array of products that changed the lives of people throughout the world. Probably the most famous and life-changing of the Edison inventions was the electric light. It was just a matter of arranging an electrical resistor so that it glowed from electrical charge and would last without burning up. Edison's efforts to find the right conditions and materials for the light are legendary. Thousands of materials were tried as resistors (he settled on a carbon filament) until the right threads produced the desired light when encased in a vacuumed bulb. The electric light was immediately accepted and was so innovative that warning signs accompanied each installation. Some of these signs still exist warning users not to try to light the light with fire but just to flip the switch on the nearby wall for illumination.

Aftermath

West Orange and General Electric. Edison's work finally outgrew the building at Menlo Park, and he moved to a larger labo-

ratory in West Orange, New Jersey. It continued to turn out hundreds of inventions of use to the growing industries of the world. Strangely, Edison did not earn any large amount of money from these inventions. But in 1892 the Edison Electric Company was sold to General Electric, and that company continued to build it into one of the largest and most effective industrial laboratories. The procedures remained the same as Edison's for many years—painstaking trial and error experiments that the famous Italian inventor Nikola Tesla describes as the needle in the haystack approach.

The $4 million Edison earned from the sale to General Electric financed other projects, but none were as successful as the electric light and the electric power plant. He returned much of what he earned into financing the careful processes he used in invention.

Mary and Mina. In 1884 Mary Edison died of typhoid, and Edison later remarried. His new wife was Mina Miller, who had made a name for herself in educational show business. By this time (1885), Edison could hardly hear. He taught Mina the Morse Code, and they talked with each other by tapping out messages on each other's hands. In Mina he had finally met someone who could get him out of his scrubby work clothes into an occasional suit suitable for society visits. Edison had always preferred to wear clothes that looked as if he had slept in them, which, indeed, he often had. Edison died in 1931.

For More Information

Bryan, George S. *Edison, The Man and His Works.* Garden City, New York: Doubleday, 1926.

Gies, Joseph, and Frances Gies. *The Ingenious Yankees.* New York: Thomas Y. Crowell, 1976.

Jehl, Francis. *Menlo Park Reminiscences.* 2 vols. Dearborn, Michigan: Edison Institute, 1927.

Silverberg, Robert. *Light for the World: Edison and the Power Industry.* Princeton, New Jersey: Princeton University Press, 1967.

◀

Thomas Alva Edison in 1888 in his chemical laboratory in West Orange, New Jersey; the nineteenth-century fury of discovery led to perhaps the most important of all the nineteenth-century inventions: the industrial laboratory.

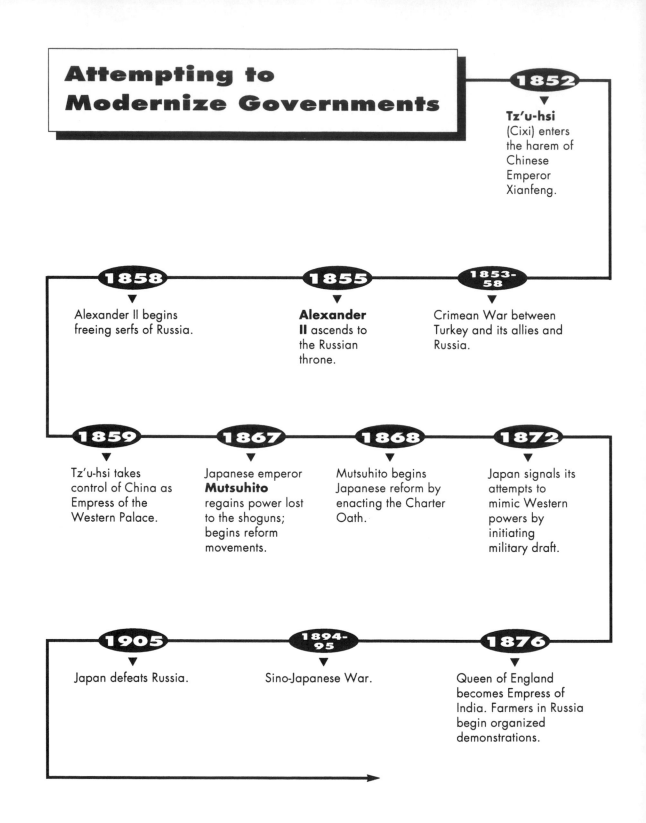

Attempting to Modernize Governments

1852
▼
Tz'u-hsi (Cixi) enters the harem of Chinese Emperor Xianfeng.

1853-58
▼
Crimean War between Turkey and its allies and Russia.

1855
▼
Alexander II ascends to the Russian throne.

1858
▼
Alexander II begins freeing serfs of Russia.

1859
▼
Tz'u-hsi takes control of China as Empress of the Western Palace.

1867
▼
Japanese emperor **Mutsuhito** regains power lost to the shoguns; begins reform movements.

1868
▼
Mutsuhito begins Japanese reform by enacting the Charter Oath.

1872
▼
Japan signals its attempts to mimic Western powers by initiating military draft.

1876
▼
Queen of England becomes Empress of India. Farmers in Russia begin organized demonstrations.

1894-95
▼
Sino-Japanese War.

1905
▼
Japan defeats Russia.

ATTEMPTING TO MODERNIZE GOVERNMENTS

By the middle of the nineteenth century the European nations were involved in a global race to establish new markets and sources of raw materials for their growing factories. The race produced an era of world reorganization. The ideas of the Enlightenment continued to influence European government reforms, while these same governments sought to create empires in Asia and Africa. The effects of this dynamic movement were to affect such distant nations as China and Japan in the East, as well as Russia, which was struggling to take its place among the great powers of Europe.

Russia and the Catholic Orthodox Church. Russia began the nineteenth century in a conservative mode. The government, along with the Orthodox Church, held the nation in a state of conservatism and lethargy for the first half of the nineteenth century, but there always existed a potential for rebellion as Russians yearned for the new-found freedoms being won in the countries of western Europe.

Because of the reactionary government's close ties to the church, Russian czars (emperors) saw themselves as protectors of Christian beliefs. By mid-century the nation's leaders felt strong enough to begin a mild expansion. Russia declared itself protector of Eastern Christians, particularly those in parts of the Ottoman Empire. Attempting this very modest expansion—to oversee Turkish Christians and protect the holy sites of Palestine—eventually brought Russia into a war with Turkey, France, England, and Sardinia. Known as the Crimean War, the conflict brought Russia defeat and the subsequent loss of some of its territory. It was evident that reform was necessary if Russia were to become a world power.

In this atmosphere, one of Russia's greatest leaders, **Alexander II,** came to power in 1855. Although he was the son of one of the country's most conservative czars, Alexander followed liberal policies and directed his efforts at leading Russia out of the age of serfdom. The 1860s saw the rise of a radicalism that had long been brewing in Russia, owing in part to the ideas of the Enlightenment, but more directly to the transformation of European societies. It was inevitable that western European revolutionary ideas would filter into a Russia that was already in decline due to internal unrest. Alexander, through the dictatorial powers he inherited as czar, directed vital reform in Russia, ordering the freeing of slaves and giving limited rights to the serfs. Nevertheless, his reforms were judged insufficient by Russian revolutionaries, and in 1881 he was assassinated. Within a few decades the entire Romanov czarist dynasty would fall to revolutionaries.

China. China, too would feel the impact of European imperialism as France and Britain both demanded that China be opened to European trade. In open warfare and through the importation of opium into China, European powers forced the Chinese nation into a struggle to preserve its dignity and identity. A powerful concubine of the Chinese emperor, **Tz'u-hsi** (also spelled Cixi), took command of the nation in 1861 and preserved its institutions for nearly fifty years. She guided the nation through its challenges from the West and from challenges for reform from the Chinese peasantry. Eventually, Tz'u-hsi came to recognize the need for reform and spent her last decade trying to bring about the end of feudalism in China.

Japanese transformation. Meanwhile, Japan had plodded along, sheltered from outside influences by a line of 120 emperors. Over the centuries, these emperors had become religious leaders, while the real government of Japan was held with iron fists by a series of warrior nobles, or shoguns, and their loyal troops, the samurai. But by the late nineteenth century the samurai had become restless under the direction of the powerful shogun. A samurai revolution overthrew the ruling shogun and restored the ancient power of government to the emperor, **Mutsuhito.** He had been raised in a conservative and comfortable household of a figurehead emperor and gave no sign of a rebellious nature until he was given power by the samurai uprising. Then, realizing the necessity of competing with or protecting Japan from European powers, Mutsuhito began a campaign of reform that would eventually transform Japan into a modern industrial nation. He adopted the Charter Oath, which transformed Japan into a politically and economically unified system of government. His actions did away with centuries of feudalism and fighting among royal clans.

Perhaps the strongest influence in Japan's transformation came from the influx of Western ideas accepted and encouraged by Mutsuhito. These ideas did much to wake up a nation that was desperate to position itself for world power. The trend has continued far into this century.

Alexander II

1818–1881

Personal Background

The Russian Empire and serfdom. The most central element of the Russian Empire under which Alexander II eventually came to power was the Russian Orthodox Church. The czars saw themselves as rulers not only by lineage but by divine right in a partnership with the church that dated back to the middle of the fifteenth century with Ivan the Great, the first czar. Prior to 1861 Russia was also a slave state. The plight of the peasantry was no mystery to any of the rulers. In 1850 about one-third of the Russian population was enslaved for reasons including being in debt, defaulting on taxes, committing a crime, or being a prisoner of war. Czar Nicholas I, Alexander II's father, was well aware of the need for social reform, but he was incapable of taking on the task. He regarded himself above all as the champion of absolutism and the divine right of rulers.

Alexander's upbringing. The Russian ruler now known as Alexander II was born on April 29, 1818, the son of the Russian czar Nicholas I. He was given the name Aleksandr Nikolayevich. A major concern of every czar was that his heir receive due preparation. Alexander was mothered by all the court women and looked after by his tutor. He was the first czar to have the history of Russia presented to him in a scholarly fashion. Alexander's tutor, Zhukovsky, organized the boy's studies around history and

▲ **Alexander II**

Event: Reforming Russian government.

Role: A man known to the world as the Czar-Liberator, Alexander II was the most liberal ruler of the Russian Romanov dynasty. The reforms he attempted were unprecedented in Russia, and his reign is often linked to the early roots of the Revolution of 1917, which marked the beginnings of the communist state and the end of czardom.

linguistics, but above all emphasized the Bible. His own interests led Alexander to become well versed in the dominant European languages.

Except for one area, there was no sign in Alexander's early life that he would be anything but the conservative, reactionary leader that his father had been. That area was the military. Normally, the teenage future czar would become an officer of the czar's guard and would be director of the nation's military schools. Neither of these activities interested Alexander much.

1848, the Year of Revolutions and anti-czardom. During 1848 a series of revolutions swept across the European continent, in which the new capitalists and the working class rebelled against the old autocratic governments that still held power. Nicholas I took the revolutionary storm in Europe as a threat against czardom, remarking that there was an increasing "criminal tendency to overthrow legitimate rulers." Because of these events, revolutionaries began to spread ceaseless propaganda against czardom and Russian institutions, propaganda that continued until the Revolution of 1917.

Participation: Reforming Russian Government

The Crimea and the question of emancipation. Alexander's father Nicholas had ruled Russia with an iron hand. He envisioned Russia guided by Orthodoxy as the universal religion and by an autocracy toward a goal of national unity. To this end, he took every opportunity to secure more territory for the empire, while maintaining control of the expanding area with such drastic measures as organizing a very effective secret police. He imagined himself the protector of Christians in the Middle East and, when an opportunity seemed to come to include Constantinople in the Christian sphere, he provoked a war with Turkey in 1853. The Crimean War proved much more difficult than he had planned. He did not foresee that Britain and France would side with Turkey. Weakened by the stress, Nicholas died in 1855, and Alexander became czar of Russia.

This was a very difficult time for Alexander II to assume the responsibilities of czar; there were troubles both outside and inside of Russia. For one thing, he had pressure from the church and nobility not to make peace with France and England but rather to exact revenge. Alexander, however, wanted peace.

To make matters worse, peasant unrest was increasing. About one-third of the Russian population was in some sort of slavery and demanding freedom. Against this, Alexander had to balance the interests of the nobility, the landowners, and the czarist tradition. If he proceeded to decree that all serfs were free, they had to be given land to survive. If they were to be given land, it would have to be taken from the landowners; in that case the landowners would have to be compensated. The aim was to keep everyone happy in order to avoid further internal struggle that could threaten the rule of the czar.

In an unprecedented move, Alexander decided to work with the nobility on the issue of emancipation. A host of provincial committees were arranged. These groups were satisfied that freeing the serfs was necessary and began to deliberate the conditions of this freedom. What resulted was a five-year struggle to appease various factions and to iron out the specific terms for emancipation.

By 1861 more than twenty-three million men were freed from serfdom. Some historians credit Alexander II with transforming Russia from a feudal state to a young democracy. Yet it was not as simple as it seemed. The conditions for emancipation in reality only produced a time bomb. Although the freed serfs were given land, it was not on an individual basis. Land was distributed through village communes. In order to finance the repayment to the landowners for their land and loss of serfs, the village communes had to collect enough taxes to repay the government. This situation perhaps created more problems than it solved. Still, Alexander's reforms were far from insignificant; they were to have far-reaching effect.

Family life. In his early twenties, Alexander had visited some of the other countries of Europe, especially the Germanic nations. On the trip, he met Maximilienne Wilhelmine Marie and, in 1841, married her. Maximilienne then became Maria Alexandrovna. She would eventually bear Alexander six sons and two daughters. The empress initially made a very favorable impression on the liberal czar due to her spirit of reform. She encouraged the education of women and was very supportive of Alexander's reform policy. Yet as the toil of reform began to drain Alexander, he became increasingly disenchanted with his wife. After the death of his mother, a very noble, pious woman, the rift in the marriage intensified, giving way to a depressing domestic life.

It was in this poor atmosphere that their son Alexander Alexandrovitch, the future heir to the throne, was raised. He witnessed the dissolution of his parents' marriage. In fact, Alexander II decidedly broke with tradition in yet another way by neglecting the education of the young heir. The boy's tutorship was left to a ruthless authoritarian who taught Alexandrovitch nothing but prejudices. This left the heir to the Russian throne unprepared and thus sowed the seeds for a future reaction against the czar's liberalism and doomed his prospects of political reform.

Polish mutiny. Civil unrest in neighboring Poland created further instability in the Russian Empire. Following the defeat of Napoléon in 1814, three of the victors—Prussia, Russia, and Austria—joined together in 1815 in the Holy Alliance and divided Poland among themselves. Immediately, the people of Poland began building a resistance against their conquerors.

In former times, under Alexander I, who had been emperor of Russia and king of Poland, the latter country had enjoyed its own parliament and a measure of independence. Polish nationalism, nevertheless, had grown and led to a massive insurrection in 1830 under Czar Nicholas I. Nicholas saw it as a major threat and crushed the rebellion, unleashing a violent Russification in Poland. It was made a Russian province, and the Russian language was forced into courts and schools. This fed further criticisms of czardom on the part of England, France, and America.

Now, under Alexander II, more amnesty was granted to Poland, though this did not quell the demands for complete emancipation. The issue generated further unrest among the Polish peasants. About 1863 an upsurge of militant nationalism, opposed to Russification, swept Poland. Shopkeepers even refused to serve customers speaking Russian. When another rebellion turned violent, Alexander II had no option but to adopt a forceful policy.

Although the insurgents were dealt with rather swiftly, a hostile Poland proved to be a drain on the Russian Empire.

Alexander and reform policy. In spite of the difficulties, Alexander remained deeply committed to reform. One of his uppermost concerns was the advancement of popular education, championed by intellectuals such as Tolstoy. Upon assuming power, Alexander made sweeping reforms in education, creating new facilities for university education and paving the way for expanded educational opportunities for Russia's people.

Alexander was also instrumental in enlarging the freedom of the press. However, these freedoms were often limited due to the increasing radicalism of the press. In addition, with the help of advisers, Alexander made significant progress in reforming the courts. He and others called for judicial impartiality and equality for all.

Plots against Alexander. Alexander's efforts to improve the lives of the average Russian sometimes produced unwanted side effects. One such reform was a change in the travel rules for Russian citizens. Czar Nicholas I had not allowed people to come and go from Russia. They seldom entered the country and usually left only when exiled. Alexander opened the doors, allowing people to travel more freely in and out of Russia. One result was that many embittered exiles returned with renewed radicalism. Many individuals also left Russia by their own choice and through their travels became exposed to Western ideals. Also in part due to Alexander's reforms in the area of education, a growing number of intellectuals emerged, posing a substantial challenge to autocratic rule.

In fact, many intellectuals, in their revolutionary zeal, sought to reeducate the peasantry, who saw the czar and God as unquestioned authorities. Among the notable intellectuals of the period were the writers Fyodor Dostoyevsky and Ivan Turgenev and the philosopher and poet Vladimir Solovyov. Some revolutionaries even sought to forcibly destroy all autocratic symbols and authoritarian institutions.

In 1862 and 1863 two plots to kill Alexander were uncovered. But it did not stop there. Numerous other attempts were carried out—four assassination attempts were put down in 1866 alone. Still, Alexander persisted in reforming and preserving Russia.

▲ Two modern Moscow schoolgirls; Alexander made sweeping reforms in education, creating new facilities for university education and paving the way for expanded educational opportunities for Russia's people.

War on Turkey. Increasing conflicts with Turkey over the sovereignty of Bulgaria forced a hesitant Alexander to declare war on Turkey in 1876. By 1878 Bulgaria was liberated. That year the Berlin Congress brought together prominent members of the European community in order to establish peace terms. There was every indication that the European community would propose a shift in the balance of power that would weaken Russia. Unfortunately for Russia, Alexander was unable to attend due to the grave condition of his dying wife.

Otto von Bismarck, the Prussian leader, dominated the hearings. Given his personal ill feelings toward Russia, joined with those of the European nations, the resulting terms of peace were very unfavorable to Russia and were consequently very unpopular among the Russian people. The injustice was exaggerated by the press, and what resulted was an even more volatile revolutionary fervor.

The terror of 1879-81. The civil unrest in Russia that followed the Berlin Congress had developed out of the suffering due to the Turkish War, the unceasing corruption in government, and the general dissatisfaction of the peasants and working class. It was a period marked by numerous savage terrorist acts. In 1881 Alexander's good fortune finally failed him. He was attacked by a revolutionary group and struck by a series of bombs in a gruesome killing.

Aftermath

The decline of the Romanov dynasty. Alexander's death marked the beginning of the end of the Romanov dynasty. His rule set in motion events that were predictable and inevitable. Alexander's reign convinced his successors that revolutionaries would never be satisfied with liberal conduct. More importantly, his reforms paved the way for a speedier modernization that would eventually climax in revolution.

A year before Alexander's death, a memorial was held on behalf of the great Russian poet, Aleksandr Pushkin. Dostoyevsky, author of such novels as *The Brothers Karamazov* and *Crime and Punishment,* was the orator. Echoing the spirit of the masses, he said that it was important to return the soil to the Russian people. This was a deep message at a critical juncture in Russian history. It was, in fact, a precursor to the Bolshevik Revolution of 1917, which brought to power Vladimir Lenin and his communist agenda with the promise of land reform.

For More Information

Graham, Stephen. *Czar of Freedom.* New Haven, Connecticut: Yale University Press, 1935.

Mosse, Werner. *Alexander II and the Modernization of Russia.* New York: Macmillan, 1958.

Smith, David. *Russia of the Czars.* London: Ernest Benn, 1971.

Mutsuhito

1852–1912

Personal Background

The Mikado as a Japanese institution. The emperors of Japan trace their claim to rule through a two-thousand-year history and more than one hundred twenty divine rulers. Over the centuries, the emperor became a symbol of Japanese unity, revered by the Japanese people but only as a figurehead. The government was run by a powerful warrior "shogun" backed by nobles known as samurai. From a political point of view, by the nineteenth century, the emperors had come to have no real authority. Rather, these "deities" were mere puppets, manipulated to serve the ends of the various clan leaders of the Japanese feudal system. Osahito, Mutsuhito's father, was the last emperor to be revered in such a manner.

The childhood of the young prince. Mutsuhito, number 121 in the line of hereditary emperors, was born in Kyoto, Japan, on November 3, 1852, the son of a royal concubine, Nii no Tsubone, and Emperor Osahito. Osahito had assumed the throne in 1845 and continued to maintain the comfortable image of a hermit Japan, sealed off from the rest of the world, particularly the encroaching Western powers. For centuries Japan had pursued isolationist policies, forbidding almost all trade with foreigners and travel to foreign lands. This changed, however, in 1854, when an American naval officer forced Japan to enter into trade with the West. Disruption of Japan's feudal system was to follow.

▲ **Mutsuhito**

Event: Reforming Japanese government.

Role: Mutsuhito, emperor of Japan, began the transformation of Japan into a politically and economically unified system of representative government, undoing centuries of feudalism and clan division.

Mutsuhito did not have the pampered, overindulgent upbringing of the typical royal child. At his father's command, he was raised in stern austerity, living a life of physical hardships. The young prince was forced to spend a great deal of time outdoors doing strenuous exercises, and in his teens he fulfilled the traditional family duty of membership in the royal guard. As a young man Mutsuhito did show some of the qualities thought necessary in an emperor. However, he must have been a disappointment to his father, for he had no real interest in the military, which his father loved. As a first son, he was also supposed to be ruler of the military schools; Mutsuhito, however, preferred to write poetry.

What's In a Name?

In the west, the man who restored the power of the emperor is called Mutsuhito, which means gentleman, and seemed fitting to the Western view of Japan's gentle but forceful leader. In Japan he was known as Tensai Sana, august son of heaven. After his death, he became Meiji Tenno, or enlightened ruler.

Still, Mutsuhito played his role as son of the emperor well. And in 1860 he was proclaimed Imperial Prince in preparation for his ascendancy to emperor. It promised to be an easy position to occupy. He would be the one hundred twenty-first divine emperor, with great wealth, esteemed by all the Japanese people. For this luxurious position, he needed to do very little—the actual work of governing Japan was the responsibility of the shogun, a military leader from the strongest of one of Japan's many clans. As he grew to be a young man, Mutsuhito gave little indication that he would not be a conservative ruler like his father.

Participation:
Reforming Japanese Government

Revolution and the beginning of the Meiji government. Osahito died at the beginning of a samurai revolt. Mutsuhito assumed the role of emperor in 1866 in the midst of clan divisions that would soon bring about the fall of the shogun and demands that the emperor take active command of the government. As he took office, Western-educated Japanese students were demanding a representative government. Tensions over the state of the existing system began to mount; the country seemed to be ready for revolution. In January 1868 the clan leaders of the southwest seized control of the palace and proclaimed emperor Mutsuhito to be the real ruler of Japan. The new emperor proclaimed the establishment of a new order in Japan, beginning with the abolition of the powerful office of the shogun, the commander in chief, and the influence of the Yedo tribe from which he came. The united clan leaders who put Mutsuhito in power envisioned a unified, strong government with an emperor who would reign and govern. A Charter Oath was written and sworn to by the emperor, symbolizing Japan's first steps toward constitutional government. This decree was formally issued in the era of the Meiji, or Enlightened, government.

Mikado?

In the West, the divine ruler of Japan was given the title *Mikado*. This term is not used in Japan. There the word for a divine ruler is *Tenno*.

The Charter Oath. The oath secured the emperor's sanction of the developing constitution. It aimed at safeguarding the nation against clan supremacy by setting up the first institution of representative government, the assembly. State policies were to be decided by "the people," a term initially limited to three groups of officers: the samurai, kuge, and daimio. This decree also demanded that all clan properties be surrendered to the emperor in one of the first moves toward centralized government. That would strike a sharp blow at the Japanese feudal system.

Feudal challenges to the new rule. Almost immediately after the issuing of the Charter Oath, clans loyal to the deposed shogun worked to overthrow the new leaders. In particular, leaders in the former stronghold of Yedo opposed relinquishing power. These rebels established a puppet ruler to rival the young emperor. However, the power and the will of the new leaders were in force, and the rebellion was quickly defeated by the emperor's troops in November 1868.

Moving from a sectarian to a national government. A number of steps were taken in the process of moving from a collection of regional, clan-controlled governments to a national, unified government. Mutsuhito ordered research directed toward establishing a national school system, as well as locating a source of revenue for these and future public expenditures. In addition, Japan took its first steps from its hermit, autocratic image, and became more active in foreign affairs by appointing its first for-

▲ In his teens Mutsuhito fulfilled his traditional family duty of membership in the royal guard.

eign minister, and shortly after, its first ambassador to the United States. Mutsuhito was convinced that Japan must take on some of the qualities of the West. The best way to do that, the emperor felt, was to copy these foreign nations.

Mutsuhito convened the first Japanese parliament in Kyoto in 1869. It was a limited step toward a representative democracy. In reality it served only a few, as clans were allowed to participate in parliament, but not the common people in cities and towns. In total, about 200 out of 276 possible samurai participated in the new body.

Redefining "the people." Mutsuhito's next step was to abandon the order of samurai altogether. In another blow to feudalism and sectarianism, the emperor issued a decree that for the first time addressed the general populace. The citizenry of Japan expanded to include both the gentry and the common people, and those who were formerly stigmatized as outcasts were to be accepted as citizens, along with the nobles. The power of the samurai, Mutsuhito felt, needed to be broken. Civil and military classes were placed on an equal footing.

Politics and religion. In the ongoing attempts of Mutsuhito and the Meiji government to defuse the power of clan separatism, Mutsuhito proclaimed Shintoism the national religion and prohibited the practice of Chinese-inspired Buddhism. Though temporarily weakened, Buddhism's strong roots in Japan allowed it to maintain its strength among its adherents.

Fear of foreign intervention and colonization led to the establishment of a national army in 1871. There was conscription at all class levels, again promoting national unity, and each clan was expected to furnish artillery and infantry to the new army.

The Japanese court system was also established in 1871, with courts divided to deal with private law and a civil code. The emperor created a tribunal (a sort of supreme court) and a court of appeals for civil and criminal cases.

During the Meiji era, foreign experts, or Yatoi, were consulted heavily to aid in the political, social, and economic construction of the new Japan. Under the guidance of these mostly American advisers, the government established an imperial treasury and began to coin money, operate an internal revenue system, and develop a postal system.

Internal strife tests the new national army. The Meiji government was never without opposition from some of the clan leaders desperately attempting to withstand the blows to the centuries-old feudal system and maintain their power. In 1871 an unsuccessful attempt was made to kidnap Mutsuhito and regain control. Two years later, the Saga rebellion tested the loyalty of the national army, when some clan leaders rushed to declare war on Korea, claiming that country had issued several insulting statements accusing Japan of befriending itself to the West. Several banks were robbed to fund the proposed military expedition. Mutsuhito decided to test Japanese loyalty. He issued rules to test the loyalties of the various rebel clan members. The rules invoked by Mutsuhito earned him the title he would worthily assume many times in the future, that of the "Peacemaker."

Not all the Japanese approved of the peaceful ruler and his reforms. In Kyushu, a bloody civil war was started by Japan's leading warrior, Saigo of the Satsuma clan, employing sixty-five thousand national troops and nearly twenty-two thousand rebel soldiers. The war began in 1877 and lasted nine months, becoming another crucial test of the new national army, which was pitted this time against many of the samurai of the old order. It was a decisive and important victory for Mutsuhito and his army.

Upholding the promises of the Charter Oath of 1868. At the insistence of up-and-coming, mostly Western-educated political reformers, the emperor and his ministers made strides to fulfill the Charter Oath of 1868, which promised to establish a truly representative national assembly. In 1888 a political system of cities, towns, and villages was organized; prefectures and counties were later included to this new body politic. In 1890 Mutsuhito finally established a Japanese Parliament, the Diet.

Later Meiji era and Japanese imperialism. When the rebellion led by the Satsuma clan was suppressed in the late 1870s, Mutsuhito and the statesmen who ruled Japan no longer had any significant opposition within their nation. After centuries of isolation and internal wars between clans, the nation was strong, unified, and prosperous, with newly Westernized industry and a powerful military. At that time the Japanese people began to recover some of their long-held traditions, such as glorifying warriors and maintaining a fierce devotion to the emperor. All of these factors led to fervent nationalism and imperialism, and during the last two decades of Mutsuhito's reign, Japan took center stage as a world power. The military, initially fortified to ensure independence from Western nations, soon became the instrument by which Japan could expand its empire throughout the East.

Japan's first military victory was in the Sino-Japanese War (1894-95; *Sino* means Chinese) from which it acquired Formosa and the Pescadores as well as a part of Manchuria. In the Russo-Japanese War (1904-05) Japan surprised the world when it quickly defeated Russia's powerful forces. During the Sino-Japanese and Russo-Japanese wars, Japanese forces had entered Korea. They never left the country, ruling it unofficially until 1910, when Japan officially annexed Korea. In the Treaty of Portsmouth, which ended the Russo-Japanese War, Japan was formally recognized as a world power. After Mutsuhito's death, the nation's imperialistic expansionism continued, creating many tensions in the East.

Aftermath

In 1869 Mutsuhito had taken a young woman named Haruko as his consort. The couple had a son, Yoshihiko. When Mutsuhito died in 1912, Yoshihiko became emperor, preserving the long chain of emperors. Yoshihiko's son, Hirohito, would be imperial leader of Japan during World War II. But by that time, the actual government would be controlled by elected officials and the parliament that Mutsuhito had initiated.

For More Information

Burks, Ardath. *The Government of Japan.* New York: Crowell, 1964.

Griffis, William F. *The Mikado: Institution and Person.* Princeton, New Jersey: Princeton University Press, 1915.

Maki, John M. *Government and Politics in Japan: The Road to Democracy.* New York: Praeger, 1962.

Tz'u-hsi

1835-1908

Personal Background

Yehenera. Lady Yehenera, the future empress, was the daughter of a Manchu, born in Peking into the family of Hweicheng, of a well-established clan. Her father, however, was an opium addict and a gambler, so the family was very poor. In order to escape the poverty of her youth, Yehenera was offered to the court as an imperial concubine at the age of sixteen. When she entered the court in 1852, Emperor I-chu was the seventh Manchu ruler to govern China and one of the weakest.

Yehenera entered the court of a decaying kingdom. For most of the century, European interests had been trying to gain a foothold in China. Foreign troops had stormed the cities up and down the long coast. They had invaded Canton and forced the Chinese to abandon their claim on Hong Kong. But perhaps the worst invasion was that of traders in opium.

Opium Wars. Beginning in 1729 the Manchu government had had a monopoly on opium, levying very high taxes on its sale. Thus only a privileged few were exposed to it. British merchants saw an incredible opportunity for profit and began dumping cheap Indian opium into the hands of the Chinese poor. The drug was so addictive that it literally changed Chinese society, undermining family life and further weakening the government. Reportedly, even eunuchs in the Manchu court were addicted. The cost of the

▲ Tz'u-hsi

Event: Attempting to modernize Chinese government.

Role: Tz'u-hsi's reign as empress in China during the latter half of the nineteenth century was marked by unending foreign invasion and internal conflict. After unsuccessfully resisting foreign presence in China by encouraging the Boxer Rebellion, Tz'u-hsi began modern reforms in China's government, military, trade, and education.

Until recently the legacy of Empress Tz'u-hsi was distorted by one of the biggest deceptions of human history. In 1974 Edmund Blackhouse, the biographer most responsible for the widespread image of the empress as a monster whose sexual desires were insatiable, was revealed to be a fraud. In 1910 he had tricked a well-known China correspondent into collaborating with him on *China under the Empress Dowager,* a work allegedly based on a Manchu official's secret diary that contained inside information.

As if this farce were not enough, the problem of finding reliable sources on much of Tz'u-hsi's life was further complicated when, in 1901, European allied forces stormed Peking, burning the recording office that housed many documents containing the real details of the empress's life.

Since 1974 historians have been trying to uncover the truth about the empress. Some of the only reliable sources include the extensive diaries of Robert Hart, a chief customs officer who resided in China and spoke the language. Other sources include unpublished correspondence between Blackhouse and George Morrison, a China correspondent for the *London Times.*

imports was so high by 1839 that not even all the Chinese export of tea could make up the lost revenue. The economic situation worsened dramatically.

The Manchus were forced to take action. Emperor Daoguang, the predecessor of I-chu, had underestimated the desire for conflict on the side of the British and French allies. The British wanted to penetrate the Manchu court and send envoys there. All the allies wanted to position themselves to get a portion of the huge empire. I-chu, however, hoped that the matter would end by his issuing a decree that condemned the European traders for bringing in illegal opium. In this decree, he referred to the Europeans as "barbarians." That was all the excuse the allies needed.

The first Opium War was from 1839 through 1842. The Manchu rulers of China were by that time ill-prepared for combat. The result was a crushing defeat, in which the emperor fled Peking and was forced to agree to the Treaty of Nanking, ratified in 1842. This treaty marked a turning point in Chinese history. It called for the opening of five posts to foreign trade, gave Hong Kong to Great Britain, and paid indemnities for war to France and Britain. But this was not the end of the opium ordeal.

By 1854 the demands by Britain, France, the United States, and Russia had increased. They called for complete legalization of the opium trade. Emperor I-chu now had to cope with the situation. Knowing well that any resistance would be met with crushing defeat, he also chose to stand firm. The result was another invasion of the palace by the allies in the

Second Opium War. The allies again coerced the Manchus into signing the Treaty of Tianjin in 1859. This treaty opened ten new ports and allowed foreigners to travel freely in the interior, including Protestant and Catholic missionaries.

The War of the Long-haired Rebels. Meanwhile, another European influence was being felt in southern China. A school-teacher had read and been influenced by European Protestant writings and had organized a rebellion to overthrow the Chinese government and Confucianism and install Christianity. The rebellion began in 1850 and grew to such size that the weak Chinese government was forced to ask the enemy Britons and French to help put it down. In all this turmoil, China might well have fallen completely apart were it not for the strength of Yehenera.

Participation: Attempting to Modernize Chinese Government

The birth of Yehenera's son and her rise to power. Shortly after the Second Opium War in 1856, Yehenera gave birth to Tsai-ch'un (also spelled Tongzhi), the son of I-chu. As the biological mother of the new heir, she achieved the highest status of a Chinese woman entering the Manchu court as a concubine. She was now second only to the emperor's first wife and was soon to change her name to Empress Tz'u-hsi (also spelled Cixi).

It was the opium conflicts that brought Tz'u-hsi into true power. The Second Opium War had forced the emperor out of Peking. During his absence, there was a struggle for power among the princes and officials of the court. All of them underestimated Yehenera. She knew that the emperor had never officially named an heir so, shortly before the death of the emperor (who was never to return to Peking), she took her son to the emperor's deathbed. Before a large audience, she exclaimed to him that she was holding his son. In 1861, just before dying, the emperor pronounced the child the new heir and Yehenera the regent, a position shared with the emperor's wife and legal mother of the young heir. Since the new emperor was just a boy, Yehenera, or Dowager Empress Tz'u-hsi as she became known, held the highest status in the Manchu court. Officially she was Empress of the Western

▲ In order to escape the poverty of her youth, Tz'u-hsi was offered to the court as an imperial concubine at the age of sixteen.

Palace, whereas the emperor's first wife was Empress of the East-ern Palace. In fact, Tz'u-hsi became so powerful that she soon took control of the Chinese government.

Power struggle in the Manchu court. While the false legacy promoted by Tz'u-hsi's biographer Edmund Blackhouse paints a picture of the empress as an all-powerful demon, she was in fact a victim of the manipulation of vengeful princes and officials. She was certainly very cunning in her treatment of the foreign invaders and in maintaining, for nearly fifty years, the stability of an empire in decline; but she was not in a position to single-handedly direct the course of the empire.

Prince Gung was perhaps the most powerful Manchu prince. He held the two most powerful positions in the clan council. While the emperor was away during the Second Opium War, Gung was the surrogate ruler, eventually settling the terms of peace with the allies. His aim to take the throne was obvious. When Tz'u-hsi made the bold move of having her child recognized as heir, he was enraged and took stronger action to secure an advantage.

But there was also Su Shun, the prime mover of the Gang of Eight, a group of militant counselors to the emperor. Not surprisingly, Su Shun also wanted to become the new emperor. What resulted was a clash between the Gang of Eight and Kung and the rest of the court. The Gang of Eight was arrested and charged with treason. Tz'u-hsi took no part in this. In the face of criticisms against Kung for the terms of peace with the allies, she rallied against him, making it unlikely that Kung could overthrow her.

The boy emperor. Tz'u-hsi chose able ministers and managed to control the Chinese government and keep activities with the foreigners to a minimum. In 1873, however, Tsai-ch'un, the son of the empress, was thought mature enough to take the throne. Tz'u-hsi had not intended to give up her power and had not trained Tsai-ch'un for the task of ruling China. She controlled him thoroughly, settling him down into a marriage she had arranged. Nevertheless, as soon as he took the power allowed him, Tsai-ch'un decided to court the Europeans and hopefully make peace with them. This alarmed Tz'u-hsi who, after three years, persuaded her son to take a trip. He never returned, nor did his wife. Rumors spread that Tz'u-hsi had done away with him; other reports claimed that Tsai-ch'un had contracted syphilis and died. At any rate, the wise Tz'u-hsi helped elect another boy emperor, Kuang Hsu (or Guangzu), essentially a puppet ruler who was not a threat to the her.

The Sino-Japanese War. In 1894 conflict over Korea brought China and Japan to war. Since this was considered an emergency, Tz'u-hsi once again reclaimed her position as the highest in command. The following year, China was defeated.

The Boxer Rebellion. Following the Japanese defeat of China, even more foreigners entered the empire trying to claim the spoils. Perhaps the most visible were the Catholic and Protestant missionaries who claimed to have a divine agenda.

The Boxers represented a revolutionary movement against the presence of the "foreign devils," especially the missionaries. An antiforeigner secret society, the Boxers grew powerful in various regions of China at the turn of the century. They were known for their violent attacks on foreigners and Chinese Christians.

The empress followed a very shrewd, double-edged policy. On the one hand, she rallied behind the Boxers, for she identified strongly with her Manchu heritage. However, in June 1900 when 140,000 Boxers besieged the Imperial City, burning down foreign legions and massacring the missionaries, she turned on many of the Boxers in order to make the peace settlements with the allies smoother. In a wise tactical move, her return to the palace—once again taken over by the allies in retaliation for the Boxer incidents—was marked by a huge imperial procession, as if the Manchu Court had been the one victorious. This psychological masterminding was one of Tz'u-hsi's strongest weapons in holding the fragile Chinese nation together.

Reform. By the beginning of the twentieth century, Tz'u-hsi had begun to realize that the old imperial China could not hold out against both internal and external demands for reform. Beginning in 1898 a group of reformers had challenged her conservative rule—even at one time taking over the palace. Tz'u-hsi recognized the need to change Chinese politics and at the same time open the country's doors to foreign trade and industry. Early in the twentieth century she began to form trade treaties with European and American companies. At the same time, she announced changes in the Chinese government, promising the people that they would be ruled under a constitution by 1916. Her old ways, however, were difficult to part with. Little came of the trade treaties before Tz'u-hsi died in 1908, and she had not lived to see the promised constitution.

Aftermath

The boy emperor and the end of the dynasty. Shortly before her death in 1908, the empress declared the young Pu Yi to be the new emperor, replacing the recently deceased Guangzu. After her death, the Manchu court divided up into factions to control the boy emperor. Yuan Shi Kai, a former general, became emperor in 1912 after Pu Yi was deceived in an attempt to save the dynasty.

By 1916, in the face of growing protests by the Chinese people, a dying Yuan abdicated the throne, officially marking the end of the Ch'ing dynasty and of the two-thousand-year-old dynastic empire. The collapse also signaled the beginning of the Chinese revolution that had begun to ferment in the Boxer uprisings. This transformation of Chinese society would eventually culminate in the People's Republic of China.

> ## Who Were the Boxers?
>
> The Boxers were a small organization of volunteer militia, supposedly organized to defend China against foreign invaders. The name is European, having been taken from the Chinese term meaning "the fist of righteous harmony."

For More Information

Haldane, Charlotte. *The Last Great Empress of China.* New York: Bobbs-Merrill, 1965.

Seagrave, Sterling. *Dragon Lady.* New York: Alfred A. Knopf, 1992.

Warner, Marina. *The Dragon Empress.* New York: Atheneum Press, 1986.

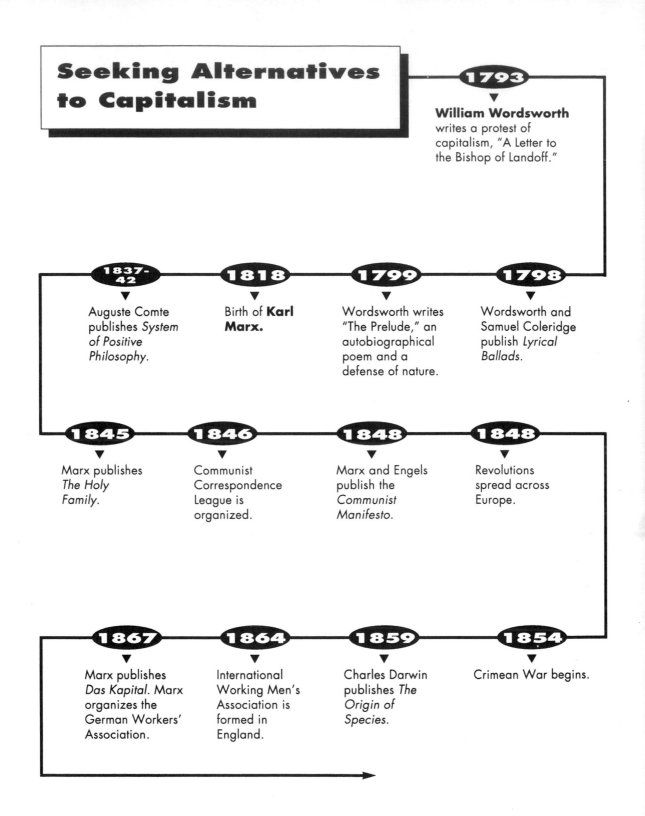

Seeking Alternatives to Capitalism

1793
▼
William Wordsworth writes a protest of capitalism, "A Letter to the Bishop of Landoff."

1837–42
▼
Auguste Comte publishes *System of Positive Philosophy*.

1818
▼
Birth of **Karl Marx.**

1799
▼
Wordsworth writes "The Prelude," an autobiographical poem and a defense of nature.

1798
▼
Wordsworth and Samuel Coleridge publish *Lyrical Ballads*.

1845
▼
Marx publishes *The Holy Family*.

1846
▼
Communist Correspondence League is organized.

1848
▼
Marx and Engels publish the *Communist Manifesto*.

1848
▼
Revolutions spread across Europe.

1867
▼
Marx publishes *Das Kapital*. Marx organizes the German Workers' Association.

1864
▼
International Working Men's Association is formed in England.

1859
▼
Charles Darwin publishes *The Origin of Species*.

1854
▼
Crimean War begins.

SEEKING
ALTERNATIVES
TO CAPITALISM

Birth of a nation. It was called a machine "that spun without fingers." John Wyatt's invention of the spinning wheel in England in 1735 signaled the beginning of the Industrial Revolution, a social and economic phenomenon that forever changed world history. Hundreds of mechanical devices were developed to aid increased production. Manufacturers and merchants discovered how abundant natural resources and elements such as coal, iron, steam, and wind could be used to cheaply operate these machines. It was also a labor revolution. Thousands of workers who had previously coupled farm work or gardening with cottage industries such as spinning cotton thread or weaving now found themselves working in large factories and living in squalid, hastily put-together city housing.

Initial effects of the Industrial Revolution. The impact of the Industrial Revolution struck first and made the greatest impression in England, which by far was the most advanced industrial society in Europe. With its great shipping fleet and access to a world market pushing for more goods, England's urban development was sudden and dramatic; within one generation, a country of farms and villages was transformed into a land of factories, mines, and cities.

▲ **An English cottage; after the Industrial Revolution thousands of workers who had previously coupled farm work or gardening with cottage industries now found themselves working in large factories and living in squalid, hastily put-together city housing.**

A second revolutionary wave followed the development of textile factories. Technology advanced with the invention of railways, steamships, telegraphs, and telephones. The wealth of the nation (and soon other nations) had long been measured by the amount of silver or gold in the corporate or government treasury. The average worker, now displaced from the farm into the large and impersonal city, seemed only to have importance as a means for the wealthy to increase their holdings. The population of destitute people increased dramatically in urban areas. Those who stayed behind in the rural areas suffered the effects of the devastating decline of domestic industries and spiraling unemployment, as well as the degradation of the natural environment.

Factories were still too new for anyone to know how best to use them. Unsanitary, dangerous work conditions and subsistence wages were the norm at many of the factories and workhouses throughout Europe. Manufacturing was a grueling job, and employees were often forced to work on the machines for hours without rest, from sunup to sundown. Even women and young children were not spared from the harshness of factory life; they were often given the worst jobs—which men refused to do—for a fraction of the pay. It was a life of disenchantment, revolving around the production of goods and backbreaking work.

Seeking alternatives to capitalism. The social and economic changes that swept Europe as a result of the Industrial Revolution led some intellectuals to examine the effects of capitalism on urban and rural life. They began to question more closely whether the economic benefits outweighed the social costs that not only the people but the environment had been forced to bear. **Karl Marx,** a German philosopher and economist, was a well known advocate for the rights of workers. In *Das Kapital,* he closely studied the social and economic effects of capitalism in England. Marx maintained that business owners were claiming as profits moneys that should have gone to the producers of the goods—the workers, or the proletariat. He recommended armed revolution on the part of the proletariat.

English poet and conservationist **William Wordsworth** celebrated the beauty of nature and rural life in his descriptions of the Lake District of northern England and the peasantry who resided there. He was well aware of the destructiveness of industrial growth. He argued for the preservation of domestic industries and railed against the rise of the factory system, which had caused a decline in the standard of living of the peasantry and an overall degradation of the environment. Wordsworth and others like him challenged nations to find ways to produce goods that would provide better conditions for the workers, while revolutionaries such as Marx sought to overthrow capitalism and substitute new management systems that promised to distribute the new wealth more evenly. Neither approach was able to stem the revolutionary social changes of industrialization.

William Wordsworth

1770-1850

Personal Background

Early childhood. William Wordsworth was born in Cockermouth, north England, in 1770, the second oldest of five children. His family was professional and solidly middle class. His father, John Wordsworth, was a lawyer for the Lowther family, wealthy landowners and a politically powerful Tory family who had made their riches by exploiting the burgeoning Industrial Revolution. The Lowthers were leading owners in the area's mining, iron ore, and shipping and building industries.

The Wordsworth children were raised in the beautiful countryside known as the Lake District, alternating between the villages of Cockermouth and Penrith, where they often stayed with their grandparents. William, along with his sister and constant companion, Dorothy, spent long periods of time outdoors, fishing and boating on the Windemere, the District's largest lake, enjoying the wilderness and basking in the splendor of nature.

This romance with nature was dampened by the death of Wordsworth's mother, Anne Cookson Wordsworth, when he was only eight years old. She died just as Wordsworth reached grammar school age, and his father sent him to the school in Hawkshead, a nearby community, where the young boy was boarded and cared for by a woman named Anne Tyson.

▲ **William Wordsworth**

Event: Protesting changes in industry.

Role: William Wordsworth is recognized as one of the world's greatest poets. Deeply affected by the ideals of the French Revolution and seeing firsthand the destruction of nature by England's industrialization, he celebrated the power and beauty of nature while calling attention to problems of man and society.

Poverty and the death of John Wordsworth. In 1783 the lives of the Wordsworth children were dramatically changed by the death of their father. Despite being employed by the wealthy and illustrious Lowther family, Wordsworth died a destitute man, leaving nothing to support his young children. Upon inquiry, it was discovered that his supposedly rather sizable estate was mostly debts owed to him by a number of people but chiefly by his employer, Sir James Lowther. Lowther refused to pay the Wordsworth family the wages he owed his lawyer. Legal proceedings against him were immediately begun and grew to an emotionally and financially draining legal battle that was to drag on for several years. Meanwhile, the children were separated, the boys living with relations in Penrith and Dorothy in Halifax.

Poetry and radicalism at Cambridge. Wordsworth enrolled at St. John's College at Cambridge University in 1787. His original intent had been to study law, following the footsteps of his late father. However, an uncle firmly encouraged the young, penniless William to become an ordained member of the clergy and secure a comfortable income, an option that he considered for a brief period of time. Wordsworth decided to follow his own course of study, a rebellious move for a poor student, concentrating on literature and European languages. He also began to write his first serious poem, called "An Evening Walk."

France. Unsure of what to do after graduating from Cambridge, he settled in London for a few months, preparing for a life in the clergy at the insistence of his demanding relatives. However, he was able to convince his brother, now a London attorney, to loan him enough money to finance a trip to France. He wanted, he claimed, to improve his French, which would enable him to get a job as a tutor upon his return. In France, he became friends with Captain Beaupry, a Royalist who had been involved in revolutionary politics and who taught him about the social and intellectual philosophy of the revolution. Wordsworth was stirred by the suffering against which the revolutionaries were struggling and he supported the ideals of equality and abolition of socially unjust laws. He sympathized with the Girondists, the more moderate of the revolutionary groups.

Radical politics in London. Wordsworth returned to London in 1793 and soon became involved in radical politics, fired by ideals of equality. He was influenced by radical pamphlets such as Thomas Paine's "The Rights of Man," and wrote a powerful, but unpublished, piece of political prose entitled "A Letter to the Bishop of Landoff," in which he denounced the social inequalities of the British monarchy and its constitution.

Wordsworth became acquainted with William Godwin, an important English radical theorist of the 1790s, whose ideals of liberty and justice were in accord with his own. He even had plans with a colleague to start a radical newspaper focusing on social reform, but was forced to abandon the project for lack of funding. He published two works, "Descriptive Sketches," a work largely sympathetic to the revolution, and "An Evening Walk," which described his beloved Lake District, receiving a lukewarm response from readers and critics. Later during his stay in London, he met Samuel Coleridge, the great poet and a constant partner throughout the earliest and most fruitful years of his literary career.

Meanwhile, Wordsworth had made another good friend in wealthy Raisley Calvert. Wordsworth took care of Raisley as he grew weaker and weaker because of tuberculosis. When Calvert discovered that he would soon die, he gave his friend a gift of about $5,000 with the request that he try to devote his time to writing. Wordsworth decided that he could do that by adding to the gift occasional fees for tutoring. He could also make a home for his sister, Dorothy.

Wordsworth first settled in Alfoxden, a town near where Coleridge lived. Both men were now writing poetry as a serious occupation. In 1798 they decided to publish their works together. Wordsworth assembled several of his poems, including "Tintern Abbey," and Coleridge contributed a long poem called "Rime of the Ancient Mariner." They called the collection *Lyrical Ballads*. The two friends, however, had no money for publishing the book. They therefore took it to a Bristol publisher, Joseph Cottle, who agreed to publish 500 copies. The books were not an immediate success. In fact, Cottle was soon forced to sell most of them, along with the rights to the poems, to another publisher, Longman. *Lyrical Ballads,* however, became one of the groundbreaking works of the nineteenth century romantic movement. In it, the poets used the ordinary language of common people and simple, natural meter—a major break from the artificial conventions of poetry at that time.

Settling in the Lake District. In 1799 William and his sister Dorothy, who was his lifelong companion, settled in Grasmere in the Lake District in the now famous "Dove Cottage." He would travel through most of Europe admiring nature, but the lure of the beautiful Lake District was too strong to resist. This love of nature is apparent in poems such as "An Evening Walk," and "The Prelude," a long autobiographical poem of his youth that he had started a year earlier. He wanted readers of his poetry to look more closely at ordinary people, specifically the rural folk, and at the splendor of nature.

A Misjudgment

Wordsworth's first book-length venture was a financial failure. In fact, when Longman bought out Joseph Cottle and an inventory of the Cottle publications was made, Longman listed *Lyrical Ballads* as "worth nothing." He eventually gave the rights to the poems back to the authors.

In that same year, Wordsworth wrote some of his most famous poems about a mysterious character named Lucy. He called this collection the "Lucy Lyrics." Still, the bulk of his poems are about his love of nature—often including barbs that called attention to the damage that was being done to both people and nature due to England's industrial revolution.

Participation: Protesting Changes in Industry

Nature and the common man. Wordsworth had seen, in the early part of his life, the beginning of the Industrial Revolution in England. British merchants had opened vast new world markets, and the demand for goods to sell had spurred the invention of machinery to be powered by wind, water, coal, and steam. The machines in turn gave rise to large factories where the new energy sources could be efficiently used. Whereas, before, hundreds of thousands of workers combined farming with industry in cottage manufacture of textiles, now these thousands flocked to the city to live in squalor and work long hours in the factories. Meanwhile, the demand for raw materials for machinery and for fuel expanded the mining industry and brought great changes to such regions as Wordsworth's beloved Lake Country.

Wordsworth became a champion of nature and rural agrarian life and cottage industry—and an opponent of capitalism. He felt that capitalism and its great factory system took people away from nature. He thought it was important to heighten the sense of community one had with nature, because it was the only way to fully realize one's humanity.

Several of Wordsworth's works harshly criticized the socio-economic effects of the Industrial Revolution, particularly on rural life. He had seen the ravages that capitalism and industrialization had had on his beloved Lake District: the local economy, based on textiles, had been destroyed by the factory system, causing a severe rise in unemployment among the workers who were the subject of many of his writings, the peasant-yeomen. The area population suffered a sharp decrease in young working men as they flocked to the industrial sectors in search of work. There was a sizable increase in the number of beggars, and many people were forced to mortgage off their lands. Beginning with the twenty poems in the first edition of *Lyrical Ballads,* much of Wordsworth's poetry either attacks industrialization directly or concludes with sharp comments about the damage to human life through the destruction of nature.

> ## A Sample of Wordsworth
>
> Through primrose tufts, in that green bower,
> The periwinkle trailed its wreaths;
> And 'tis my faith that every flower
> Enjoys the air it breathes.
>
> (from "Lines Written in Early Spring" in Ansorge, p. 640)

"The Ruined Cottage" is another work that deals with the effects of the factory system—this time on the weaver, another profession that was on the decline in the Lake District. A direct attack on capitalism, the poem describes how the weaver, becoming more and more depressed with his seemingly permanent unemployment, slowly becomes dependent on the piecemeal wages offered by the capitalists in his search for a "purse of gold."

Wordsworth condemned the capitalist system as a danger to morals; he believed it negatively affected family life and exploited child and female labor. His poem/play entitled "The Borderers" deals explicitly with the sale of children as mere economic exchange in an uncaring market.

"The Excursion" is one of Wordsworth's most direct indictments of the effects of the capitalist system on workers. In this piece, Wordsworth's wanderer describes the changing face of England—the growth of towns and cities and the pouring of country labor into the factories. Such a system, the wanderer points out, can only lead to the intellectual degradation of the workers, with these human beings becoming mere tools of the factory. Wordsworth dramatically illustrated the effects of factory labor in an image of a young man emerging from a mill, his clothes covered with soot, his figure stooped and eyes dulled and languid.

Wordsworth Opposing Industrialization

If this belief from heaven be sent,
If such be Nature's holy plan,
Have I not reason to lament
What man has made of man?

(from "Lines Written in Early Spring" in Ansorge, p. 640)

Wordsworth's efforts at conservation. Wordsworth did attempt to use his poetry to persuade those in power to consider the devastating effects of industrialization on rural life and the peasantry. In 1801 he sent a copy of *Lyrical Ballads* to a politician, to no avail. He was more successful in 1844, when he mounted a campaign to prevent a railroad from being built through the Lake District.

Aftermath

Wordsworth's later conservatism. Though Wordsworth was progressive in his stance concerning the condition of the peasantry and of nature, his views on national politics took a decidedly conservative turn in the early nineteenth century in comparison with the radicalism of his youth. The rise of the dictatorship of French emperor Napoléon Bonaparte dashed his idealistic hopes for the revolution, and he became increasingly patriotic. He began to favor England and its institutions such as the church and the aristocracy, as long as the subjects were treated with kindness. Ironically, he even became a loyal Tory (a member of the conservative political party) and established relations with the infamous Lowther clan, who by this time had paid the Wordsworth family their due inheritance.

Marriage. In 1802 Wordsworth married his childhood play-mate and cousin, Mary Hutchinson. She, sister Dorothy, and a growing number of Wordsworth children would live happily in Dove Cottage until the poet died in 1850. Wordsworth feared the reforms that he predicted the Whigs (British liberals) would bring when they swept into power in 1832; he preferred the status quo to rabble-rousing reformers who disturbed the old order. Perhaps he had become a part of the status quo himself, having accepted a government position as distributor of stamps in 1813. From then on, life in the Wordsworth household was more secure and peaceful.

Wordsworth's new celebrity. Although scholars date his most creative period from the 1790s to the early 1800s, it was during his later years that he achieved the greatest popularity and respect, from readers and critics alike. *Lyrical Ballads* was published in its third edition. In addition, Wordsworth was having more ease in getting works published, and his audience of admirers included none other than the Queen Victoria herself. He was named poet laureate in 1843, following in the footsteps of fellow Lake Poet and friend, Robert Southey.

Wordsworth outlived the other great poets of the period with which he was identified, including the romantics, Percy Bysshe Shelley, John Keats, and George Gordon, Lord Byron, and the Lake Poets, Coleridge and Southey. The last project, and one of the most important he worked on near his death, was the production of the Fenwick notes. These were notes that he dictated to friend and Lake District neighbor, Isabelle Fenwick, on the background of his poetry, as well as the circumstances in which the poems were written.

Wordsworth died at Dove Cottage in 1850 at the age of eighty.

For More Information

Ansorge, Elizabeth, and others, editors. *Prose and Poetry of England,* New York: Singer, 1943.

Clutterbuck, Nesta, editor. *William Wordsworth, 1770-1850.* Grasmere: Dove Cottage Trustees, 1970.

Darbishire, Helen. *Wordsworth.* London: Longman Press, 1953.

Davies, Hunter. *William Wordsworth: A Biography.* New York: Atheneum Press, 1980.

Karl Marx

1818-1883

Personal Background

1818–35, the early years. Karl Marx was born and raised as a child in Trier, a German town on the Moselle River near Koblenz. Once a garden spot of the Roman Empire, the beautiful city surrounded by groves and vineyards was still, in 1818, a pleasant town of fifteen thousand inhabitants, even though the recent years had left the people there with considerable uncertainty. Conditions were particularly uncertain for the Jewish residents there, and the Marx family was a family of Jewish rabbis.

Fifteen years earlier, Napoléon Bonaparte had taken over the region of small German states and organized them into the Confederation of the Rhine. He had given the Jews there hope of more equal treatment but had placed restrictions on the kinds of work and land ownership the Jews could enjoy. Ten years later, only a few years before the birth of Karl Marx, Napoléon was defeated and the land along the Rhine and Moselle Rivers fell to Prussia.

Amid talks of revolution and promises of a constitution protecting the rights of the peasants, the emperor of Prussia worked diligently to restore the old noble-serf traditions and along with those traditions, the ancient hatred and distrust of Jews. Heinrich Marx, Karl's father, a lawyer, had already abandoned much of his family's Jewish tradition to follow deist ideas (belief in God but not in organized religious groups). So, when the Prussians

▲ Karl Marx

Event: Developing the Socialist system.

Role: A well-recognized philosopher, Karl Marx is best known as an early definer of socialism. The *Communist Manifesto,* co-written with Friedrich Engels, and *Das Kapital* describe the socialist state and became the guides for the development of the communist system. Marx continued his campaign for socialism by organizing one of the first labor unions, the International Workingmen's Association.

refused to relieve the restrictions on Jews, he simply declared his religion to be Lutheran. One year before Karl's birth, Heinrich and his wife Henrietta asked to be entered into the local Lutheran Church (although Henrietta refused baptism until her own parents died). It was into this family that Karl was born May 5, 1818. He was the oldest son and second of eight children in the Marx family.

Early in Karl's life, Heinrich recognized that his son was unusual. For one thing, he was very bright and very interested in learning. For another, even as a child he was stubborn, independent, and domineering. He attended the local schools but appeared not to be interested in mathematics or any other subjects that might prepare him to follow his father's career. Instead, Karl's best school subjects were literature and art.

When Karl was seventeen, Heinrich decided that the boy had accomplished all that he could in the local schools and should enroll at the University at Bonn. There is little evidence that Karl excelled in studies at the university. We know that he was very social, joining the other young men in drinking parties and carousing—at least once carrying on so that he was arrested. After a year at Bonn, he left the Rhine region to study at the University of Berlin, then one of the most impressive universities in all of Europe. It was at Berlin that Karl became a serious student and began to form the ideas that would later shake the foundations of many governments.

The idealist tradition. Marx studied for five years at the University of Berlin, where he was admitted into the Faculty of Law. But the dominant study at the University was philosophy, particularly the philosophy of Georg Wilhelm Friedrich Hegel (1770-1831). Marx became increasingly interested in this philosophy and its political significance. Hegel thought all of history was a series of clashes between conflicting ideas. In such changing situations, the state was an important balance. But, Hegel thought, the mass of the people should be represented in government, and their rights protected by freedom of the press and a recognized constitution giving each citizen, among other rights, the right to trial by jury and the right to free enterprise. While much

▲ Georg Wilhelm Friedrich Hegel; while much impressed by Hegel's ideas, Marx would later challenge some of them—as he was prone to challenging the thinking of most other scholars.

impressed by Hegel's ideas, Marx would later challenge some of them—as he was prone to challenging the thinking of most other scholars.

Marriage. Two men deeply influenced Marx—his father and a wealthy local government official in the Rhineland, Frieherr Ludwig von Westphalen. Westphalen was a liberal politician, much concerned with the welfare of the citizens he governed.

From these two, the young Marx had learned concern for others and the necessity of accepting change. But there was another attraction at the Westphalen home—Westphalen's daughter Jenny. In 1837, while still a student at Bonn, Marx asked for Jenny's hand in marriage and her father agreed. Six years later Jenny and Karl were married. Although accustomed to wealth and comfort, Jenny would support Marx throughout her life, even though their growing family was sometimes on the verge of starvation and they were forced to sell their furniture to get food. Through the years, the couple would have six children, although three of these would die very young, their deaths possibly hastened by the poor conditions under which the family was forced to live.

The young Hegelians. At the University of Berlin there arose a group of young men who chose to interpret the teachings of Hegel as a call to immediate reform. Marx began meeting with this group, paying much attention to conversations about religion. There was at that time a great deal of religious dispute as Lutheranism grew and Catholicism tried to hold its place. Marx began to include organized religion and even belief in a God on a level with the Prussian government and the old feudalism as barriers to human improvement. He declared himself an atheist.

At the same time, Marx began to search for the answers to human economic inequalities. He wrote his doctoral thesis about two ancient "materialists," philosophers who focused on physical objects. Democritus (c. 460-c. 370 B.C.) and Epicurus (c. 341-270 B.C.) were Greek philosophers who were among the earliest materialists. Above all, they regarded the material world as the ultimate reality. Democritus originated the theory of atoms, too small to be seen, and insisted that science should concern itself with the investigation of the innumerable phenomena of the material world. Human peace and prosperity could only be gained by focusing on the real, physical world. Marx was becoming a materialist.

Throughout the years, there had been other materialists, some of whom had begun to think of a world constantly in crisis over economic problems, with a dominant aristocracy constantly struggling with a poorer majority. Marx followed this path in his

▲ Friedrich Engels; on their first meeting, Marx and Engels shared observations for ten hours. After that, the two would work together throughout their lives.

philosophical studies, finally trying to account for all of history as a sort of class conflict between haves and have-nots.

Editing and Friedrich Engels. After earning his doctorate, Marx would probably have become a university instructor, but such an option was not available to one who openly claimed to be an atheist. Instead, he took a position as editor of the *Rheinische Zeitung,* a publication that was originally intended to protect the political and economic interests of Rhineland's trade and commerce. During this time, Marx became increasingly aware of the problems in contemporary society. As his concern for the economic inequality of those around him grew, his editorials in the paper angered more and more people, and he was forced to leave his job.

Marx then moved, in 1843, to Paris, where he met the man who would be most important to him throughout his adult life—Friedrich Engels (1820-1895). It was reported that on their first introduction, the two shared observations for ten hours. After that, Marx and Engels would work together throughout their lives. Engels was the son of a wealthy cotton merchant who had factories on the European continent and in Great Britain. While visiting one of these factories in Scotland, Engels had met a young woman worker and received firsthand accounts of the miserable conditions of British factory workers. Engels had then moved to Paris to write about the plight of workers and to work as an editor. He and Marx shared many ideas about how to correct the problems.

Marx Versus Hegel

German philosopher Georg Wilhelm Friedrich Hegel believed that reality existed only in the mind, not in the outside world. Ideas were therefore more important than physical things. He thought progress throughout history occurred when two opposing ideas clashed and gave rise to a new, better idea. This view is called dialectical idealism.

Marx accepted Hegel's method of thinking, but not his belief that ideas make up what is reality. Marx believed that reality existed in the physical world. His philosophy, called dialectical materialism, presumed that economics determine the progress of history. In Marx's view, the struggle between social classes, not ideas, brought about progress in the form of new economic systems.

They began what would amount to a forty-year collaboration, and Marx became increasingly involved in a number of decidedly socialist, or communist organizations.

Participation: Developing the Socialist System

Rejecting capitalism. By 1845 Marx had written so much calling for change in Prussia that he was not popular with the government there. The Prussians took their case to the French, and soon Marx found he was not welcome in Paris, either. Marx then left for Brussels, where, for the next couple of years, he would develop his ideas about an alternative to capitalism. In 1845 he wrote *The Holy Family,* in which he defined the course of freedom (or lack of it) under capitalism. He charged that capitalist society—with its emphases on private ownership of property, industry, and religion—is inhumane and amounts to slavery. He maintained that manufacturing and trade need to work together to affect the output of the factories; often even these divisions of the forces of production are in competition for profits (which were really the "property" of the workers). Cooperation, rather than competition, in his opinion, should be the rule.

The Communist Correspondence Committee and the Communist League. Engels subsequently joined Marx in Brussels, where they founded the Communist Correspondence Committee in 1846. The goal of the committee was to foster ties between French, British, and German socialists. The following year, both men moved to London, where they joined the League of the Just, which later became the Communist League. Engels and Marx soon assumed a leadership role in the organization. They went on to draft the "Principles of Communism" for the Second Congress of the Communist League—essentially the organization's mission statement. In the same year, Marx organized the German Workers' Association of Brussels.

> ### An Odd Assemblage of Communists
>
> Perhaps strangely, the original members of the Communist League were overwhelmingly intellectuals and professionals. Thus it was not the Marxist ideal of a worker-controlled movement. The League became an organization to do something for the workers rather than to involve the workers in doing for themselves.

Defining communism. In 1848 Marx and Engels published the *Communist Manifesto.* In it the two declared a plan to oppose capitalism. In Marx's view, capitalism forced unwanted changes in society—change guided by technological rather than human improvement. The changing technologies of evolving industry led to corresponding changes in the way people were organized for production. In the changing technology, the experiences of the owners, differing from those of the workers, created clashes of ideas, and political conflict was the inevitable result between those devoted to existing institutions and those wanting to make drastic changes. Marx believed that it was the workers' role to encourage and direct changes in society. The

Manifesto was a call for workers to organize, but at the time of its publication, Europe was involved in another form of revolution—a union of both workers and owners against the oppressive autocratic governments then dominating the continent.

Organizing the workers of England. While the Central Bureau of the Communist League in London, rebuilt by Marx in 1849, broke up two years later, the International Working Men's Association, a new organization that he founded in 1864, grew, partly because of the victories of the workers of England. These victories were small; in the association's statement of the purpose, Marx makes specific mention of goals still to be reached—the ten-hour working day and building a cooperative movement.

Das Kapital I, exploitation, and the basis for transformation. In 1867 Marx published the second of his two discussions of communism, *Das Kapital,* or in English, *Capital.* Most of the research that went into the first volume of this work was done by Marx during the 1850s while he was destitute in the London slums. In fact, it was during this period that three of his children died, possibly due to the pitiful living conditions. Still, Marx had persisted in his study and writing.

Das Kapital focused on the capitalist mode of production in England. Marx invented a new term to describe what was happening. The difference between what a product could be sold for and what was paid to the worker who made the product was, Marx said, "surplus value." In a capitalist system, Marx contended, the owner of the means of production took this "surplus value" as profit; thus, the worker could never be paid the exact worth of his or her labor. Also, as the "surplus value" accumulated in the hands of a few owners, the demand for wage workers would grow. The more workers who were not sharing in the surplus value, the greater the accumulation of capital in the hands of an increasingly smaller number of capitalists. Unrest

Communist Manifesto in Brief

In their famous call to communism, Marx and Engels proposed: 1) abolishing private ownership of property, 2) providing free education and abolishing child labor, 3) abolishing all rights of inheritance, 4) combining agriculture with manufacturing, 5) confiscating all property of rebels, 6) compelling everyone to work at state-assigned jobs, 7) placing all the means of financing industry in the hands of the state, and 8) nationalizing (giving the state control of) the means of communication and transportation.

would increase as smaller capitalists were forced to abandon their manufacture and join the ranks of the workers. To achieve a reasonable standard of living, therefore, workers needed to control the means of production—to own the factories through their participation in government.

Marx's most burning criticism of capitalist society was that it forced the laborer into existing for the sole purpose of expanding capital, instead of providing a means by which capital could be used to satisfy the needs and development of the worker. The only solution, he claimed, was for workers to join in a struggle to destroy the capitalist mode of production.

Finally, Marx made a case for his revolution by asserting that capitalism was one step along the way toward communism. Capitalism, in fact, had taken the first step toward socialism and communism by challenging the older feudal order. That having been accomplished, the time was right for the next step—forming a government that could educate the people for cooperation rather than competition, and placing all the means of production in the hands of that government. Eventually, Marx thought, cooperation would replace competition as the driving force of industry and there would be no need for a powerful government. Sharing equally in the surplus value would bring out the good that was inherent in all people.

Aftermath

Engels writes Volumes II and III. Following Marx's death in 1883, Engels published the second and third volumes of *Capital*. There is considerable debate as to what degree these texts represent the work of Marx. The worth of Volume II, which contains a discussion of reproduction and an input-output analysis, is thought to be questionable and inarguably boring. The third volume, published in 1894, is considered valuable for its perspectives on economic history.

Leninism and the first communist state. At the turn of the twentieth century, Russia was engaged in a struggle against the oppressive rule of the czars. Vladimir I. Lenin emerged as the man responsible for transforming Marxism into the basis for the rise of the world's largest and first communist state, the Soviet Union. A workers' revolution took place in Russia, but not the revolution envisioned by Marx or Engels. They had dreamed of a peaceful revolution begun by increased worker involvement in a democratic form of government. In this way, a slow-paced revolution would allow time for the workers to become more politically aware and more capable of handling the change to economic equality.

Lenin made changes in the Marxist philosophy designed to hasten the change to communism. The first of these had to do with political consciousness among the workers. Rejecting the Marxist notion that these laborers would develop political effectiveness throughout decades of struggle, Lenin reduced the time scale and declared that political consciousness would be brought to the workers, or the proletariat, from without, namely by the intellectuals and professionals who made up the earlier communist organizations. Secondly, Lenin insisted that revolution under czarist absolutism had to be secret and thus undemocratic to be successful. He associated a democratic environment with publicity and openness.

While communism in Russia ultimately failed, at least for a time, Marx's ideas found their way to other nations, and other forms of communism have been adopted as an alternative to Western capitalism.

For More Information

Elster, John. *An Introduction to Karl Marx.* Cambridge, England: University of Cambridge Press, 1986.

Gemkow, Heinrich. *Karl Marx: A Biography.* Dresden: Verlag Zeit im Bild, 1968.

Marx, Karl. *Capital: A Critique of Political Economy, Volume One.* New York: Vintage Books, 1977.

Sowell, Thomas. *Marxism: Philosophy and Economics.* New York: William Morrow, 1985.

Steele, David Ramsey. *From Marx to Mises: Post-capitalist Society and the Challenge of Economic Calculation.* La Salle: Open Court, 1992.

Bibliography

Baglehole, John Caute. *The Life of Captain James Cook*. Stanford, California: Stanford University Press, 1974.

Bekerman, Gerard. *Marx and Engels*. Translated by Terrell Carver. New York: Blackwell, 1986.

Buck, Pearl. *Imperial Woman*. New York: J. Day, 1956.

Burshell, S. C. *Age of Progress*. New York: Time Books, 1966.

Burton, H. W. *Memoirs of the Life and Labours of the Late Charles Babbage*. Pennsylvania: MIT Press, 1957.

Chamberlain, John. *The Roots of Capitalism*. Revised edition. Princeton, New Jersey: D. Van Nostrand Co., 1965

Clary-Aldruzin, Alfonse. *A European Past: Memoirs*. New York: St. Martin's Press, 1978.

Darwin, Charles. *The Origin of the Species By Means of Natural Selection; The Descent of Man and Selection in Relation to Sex*. Chicago: Encyclopaedia Britannica, 1990.

Darwin, Charles. *The Voyage of Charles Darwin*. New York: Mayflower, 1979.

Darwin, Charles. *The Voyage of the Beagle*. New York: Collier, 1909.

Desmond, Adrian, and James Moore. *Darwin: The Life of a Tormented Evolutionist*. New York: Norton, 1991.

Dmytryshyn, Basil. *USSR: A Concise History*. New York: Charles Scribner's Sons, 1978.

Dubbey, J. M. *The Mathematical Work of Charles Babbage*. Cambridge, England: Cambridge University Press, 1978.

Egan, Louise. *Thomas Edison: The Great American Inventor*. New York: Barron's Educational Service, 1987.

Faraday, Michael. *Experimental Researches in Electricity*. New York: Dove, 1965.

Fisher, Douglas Alan. *The Epic of Steel*. New York: Harper and Row, 1963.

Florence, Ronald. *Marx's Daughters: Eleanor Marx, Rosa Luxemburg, Angelica Bala*. New York: Dial, 1975.

Footman, David. *The Alexander Conspiracy: A Life of A. I. Zhelyabov*. LaSalle, Illinois: Open Court, 1968.

Fromm, Erich. *Beyond the Chains of Illusion: My Encounters with Marx and Freud*. New York: Simon and Schuster, 1962.

Gooding, David, and Frank James. *Faraday Rediscovered: Essays on the Life and Work of Michael Faraday, 1791–1867*. Basinstoke, England: Macmillan Press, 1985.

BIBLIOGRAPHY

Graham, Stephen. *Tsar of Freedom.* New Haven, Connecticut: Yale University Press, 1935.

Gray, William R. *Voyages to Paradise: Exploring in the Wake of Captain Cook.* Washington, D.C.: National Geographic, 1981.

Hough, Richard Alexander. *The Last Voyage of Captain James Cook.* New York: Morrow, 1979.

Hyman, Anthony. *Charles Babbage: Pioneer of the Modern Computer.* Princeton: Princeton University Press, 1982.

Josephson, Matthew. *Edison: A Biography.* Norwalk, Connecticut: Easton, 1986.

Kippes, Andrew. *Captain Cook's Voyages, With an Account of His Life, During the Previous and Intervening Periods.* New York: Knopf, 1924.

Krache, Enno. *Metternich's German Policy, 1814–1815.* Princeton, New Jersey: Princeton University Press, 1983.

Marx, Karl, and Friedrich Engels. *The Communist Manifesto.* Translated by Samuel Moore. New York: Washington Square Press, 1964.

Marx, Karl, and Friedrich Engels. *On Revolution.* New York: McGraw-Hill, 1971.

McLellan, David. *Karl Marx.* New York: Viking, 1975.

McLellan, David. *The Young Hegelians and Karl Marx.* New York: Frederick A. Praeger, 1969.

Mehring, Franz. *Karl Marx: The Story of His Life.* London: Allen and Unwin, 1966.

Mosse, Werner. *Alexander II and the Modernization of Russia.* New York: Macmillan, 1958.

Muller, Jerry Z. *Adam Smith in His Time and Ours: Designing the Decent Society.* New York: Free Press, 1993.

Nicolle, Jacques. *Louis Pasteur: The Story of His Major Discoveries.* New York: Basic Books, 1961.

Padover, Saul Kussiel. *Karl Marx: An Intimate Biography.* New York: McGraw-Hill, 1978.

Palmer, Alan. *Metternich: A Biography.* New York: Harper and Row, 1972.

Rienits, Rex. *The Voyages of Captain Cook.* New York: Hamlin, 1968.

Rogge, Benjamin A. *Can Capitalism Survive?* Indianapolis, Indiana: Liberty Press, 1976.

Scherr, Marie. *Carlotte Corday and Certain Men of the Revolutionary Torments.* New York: Appleton, 1928.

Skelton, Renee. *Charles Darwin and the Theory of Natural Selection.* Hauppage, New York: Barron's, 1987.

Smith, David. *Russia of the Tsars.* London: Ernest Benn, 1971.

Spry-Leverton, Peter. *Japan.* New York: Facts on File, 1988.

Suchting, A. *Marx: An Introduction.* New York: New York University Press, 1983.

Wordsworth, William. *Poems.* Selected by Elinor Parker. New York: Crowell, 1964.

Wordsworth, William. *The Complete Poetical Works of William Wordsworth.* Edited by Andrew J. George. Boston: Houghton Mifflin, 1972.

Index

Bold indicates entries and their page numbers; (ill.) indicates illustrations.

Profiles in World History
Significant Events and the People Who Shaped Them